A TEEN'S GUIDE TO

GETTING PUBLISHED

SECOND EDITION

SECOND EDITION

A TEEN'S GUIDE TO
GETTING PUBLISHED

PUBLISHING FOR PROFIT, RECOGNITION, AND ACADEMIC SUCCESS

Jessica Dunn & Danielle Dunn

Prufrock Press Inc.
Waco, Texas

ISBN-13 978-1-59363-182-6
ISBN-10 1-59363-182-0

Printed in the United States of America.

At the time of this book's publication, all facts and figures cited are the most current available. All telephone numbers, addresses, and Web site URLs are accurate and active. All publications, organizations, Web sites, and other resources exist as described in the book, and all have been verified. The authors and Prufrock Press Inc., make no warranty or guarantee concerning the information and materials given out by organizations or content found at Web sites, and we are not responsible for any changes that occur after this book's publication. If you find an error, please contact Prufrock Press Inc.

Dunn, Jessica, 1980–
  A teen's guide to getting published : publishing for profit, recognition, and academic success / Jessica Dunn & Danielle Dunn.—2nd ed.
    p. cm.
  Danielle Dunn's name appears first on the earlier edition.
  ISBN 1-59363-182-0 (pbk.)
  1. Authorship—Marketing. 2. Authorship. I. Dunn, Danielle, 1980– II. Title.
  PN161.D86 2006
  808'.02—dc22

                        2006005109

Prufrock Press Inc.
P.O. Box 8813
Waco, TX 76714-8813
Phone: (800) 998-2208
Fax: (800) 240-0333
http://www.prufrock.com

For Hubert Berg
A man loved by so many,
especially those privileged
to call him Grandpa.

CONTENTS

• • • • • • • • • • • • • • • • •

Introduction: Why Publish?   1

Chapter 1: The Writing Craft   5
The Writer's Toolbox   5
Finding Inspiration   7
Prose, Poetry, and Puzzles   11
Editing Techniques to Improve Your Writing   19

Chapter 2: Freelance Publishing   25
Selecting Your Targets   25
Preparing Your Submission   28
Rights and Copyright   40
Online Publishing   45
Tracking Your Progress   51
The Unfortunate Realities of Freelancing   55
Pitfalls of Publishing   60

Chapter 3: Getting Feedback   67
Getting the Most From Feedback   67
Mentors   71
Professional or Peer Critique   73
Correspondence Programs   81
Writing Camps and Workshops   84
Writers' Clubs   87

Chapter 4: Beyond Freelancing   91
    School Publications: Yearbooks, Newspapers,
        and Literary Magazines   91
    Writing a Column   94
    Writing for Local Newspapers   99
    Becoming an Editor   112
    What About Book Publishing?   127
    Self-Publishing   139

Chapter 5: (Not Your Ordinary) Directory of Markets   143
    Publications: Print and Online   143
    Markets to Watch   191
    Contests   196
    Note About Contests   221

Epilogue   223

Appendix A: Regional and National Writing Camps   225

Appendix B: Book Publishing Opportunities   235
    Contests   235
    Mainstream Book Publishers   241

Additional Resources   243
    Books   243
    Web sites   244

About the Authors   249

ACKNOWLEDGEMENTS

• •

We would especially like to thank our publisher Joel McIntosh for taking a chance on this book 10 years ago, and our editor Jennifer Robins for the hours of work she put into preparing this second edition for publication. Also, thanks to the rest of the staff at Prufrock Press for their efforts. A special thanks goes to our family, and particularly our parents, Kathy and Bryan Dunn, for their enthusiasm and unwavering support. We remember and appreciate the encouragement and wisdom from our English teachers over the years, especially Barbara Stern, Betty Ann Williams, Alaine Butz, and Marsha Sachs, who each played a role in shaping us into the writers we have become. Last, but most certainly not least, our sincere thanks to you for giving this book a try. We hope you will find it helpful and enjoy reading it as much as we enjoyed writing it. Best of luck to you.

PROLOGUE

● ● ● ● ● ● ● ● ● ● ● ● ● ● ● ● ● ● ●

Dear Jessica and Danielle, . . . I am very interested in publishing your book. I think [it] will be an excellent addition to our line of editorial products. . . . I can extend to you a royalty of 10% of net book sales. . . .

Writers everywhere dream about receiving a letter that looks something like this. When Prufrock Press wrote these words to us in February 1995, neither of us could believe it. We were 14 years old. A genuine publisher actually wanted to publish our book! How had we managed to attain this opportunity?

OK, back up a few years. At age 12, we both enjoyed composing short stories and poems to share with our family and for our own amusement. Our journey into print began at a book fair, where we met Ms. Ethel Evey, a writer who was there signing and selling her books. When we expressed an interest in writing, Ms. Evey promised to send us a list of magazines that published work by children. This really excited us because the only magazines we had heard of didn't take work from "amateur" kids and teens. Ms. Evey warned us that the list was very short and so old that some of the magazines might have gone out of business, but that didn't matter. It was a start.

For some time after receiving the list, we went to the library several times a week looking for additional markets. Over the next couple of years, each of us managed to get a handful of poems and several puzzles published in magazines like *Creative Kids* and *Merlyn's Pen*. We learned a lot from each exhilarating success, and even more from the many rejections. Oddly, neither of us can remember exactly how we got the idea to write this book. Still, once the idea presented itself, we both dove into the project. As the manuscript grew, we began to entertain the wild idea of submitting it to a publisher. Having had work printed in *Creative Kids*, we first thought of its publisher, Prufrock Press. Neither of us will ever forget the day that Prufrock said "yes" to our manuscript—and that was just the beginning. After months of revisions under the expert guidance of Prufrock editor Stephanie Stout, the finished book debuted in April 1996, when we were 15 years old.

Since then, we have both found ways to stay involved in writing and publishing. We wrote several articles together, including a column for *Young Entrepreneur Newsmagazine*, during high school. Jessica joined the yearbook staff in high school and college, while Danielle spent two summers working as a reporter for a Houston-area weekly newspaper, the *Fort Bend/ Southwest Sun*.

Although neither of us ultimately chose a career as a full-time writer (at least not so far), we both continue to enjoy writing, and use our writing skills frequently in our jobs as engineers. We were also ecstatic when Prufrock Press offered us the opportunity to revise this book and produce a second edition, 10 years after the publication of the first. It has grown tremendously—we've added sections on topics such as online publishing, becoming an editor, finding a writing mentor, and journalism, to name a few. (We have also removed all references to typewriters and expanded the vocabulary to include terms such as *blog* and *hypertext*. Technology has progressed exponentially in the last 10 years.) We hope this book will be a dependable resource for you as you venture into publishing. Good luck!

INTRODUCTION: WHY PUBLISH?

· ·

Because it's only the most rewarding hobby in the world, with prestige and accomplishment written all over it! But, you were probably looking for some actual, thoughtful reasons, not just sheer exuberance. OK, that's fair. If you're a skeptic, questioning whether the benefits really outweigh the time, effort, and risks, then let us reassure you—it's so worth it. Even if you are already certain that having your work published is something you want to do, take a few minutes to reflect on what exactly you hope to gain from this experience. It will help you keep your perspective through your successes and setbacks.

So seriously, why publish? For starters, it is a delightfully unique hobby. Lots of kids and teens do enjoy writing, but few throw themselves into publishing with real gusto (or even at all). As far as we knew, none of our other classmates in junior high and high school were doing this, which made publishing one way for us to distinguish ourselves from the crowd.

For those who love to write, publishing is also a confidence booster like no other. Seeing one's writing in print is a very rewarding experience at any age, but can be particularly beneficial for young scribes trying to assess their own level of talent. Getting published is the ultimate compliment, an affirmation that your work has strong merit. Who wouldn't find that extremely motivating? Publishing also enhances self-esteem by helping you prove to yourself, and to others, that you don't have to be attractive, popular, athletic, or even book-smart to be an interesting, talented person.

Aside from writing ability, publishing in and of itself is also a skill. It's about the buzz of matching your creative work with the right publication, the joy of finding your niche, the perfect mouthpiece for your voice. Maybe you have a fabulous imagination, a penchant for fiction or poetry, and a literary journal is just what you need to express your *joie de vivre* (French for the *joy of life*). Or, perhaps you're upset about world events or the struggles of adolescence, and you're looking for a way to scream from the rooftops without disturbing the neighbors. Outlets exist for that, too. Finding the one that speaks your language is an awesome feeling.

But, publishing is not just about giving you a chance to speak; it's also about offering others the chance to listen, and convincing them to do it. Through your writing, you can inspire, comfort, motivate, inform, or simply entertain people. Let your peers know that they are not alone in coping with blended families, cliques at school, pressure to fit in, and college applications. Or, remind them to celebrate the pleasures of youth, friendship, or escaping into a good story.

You also become a small part of history this way, contributing your own two cents to the very complicated picture of what it's like to be a teen in today's world. Seize this opportunity to show often-skeptical adults that the word *teenager* is not a synonym for *slacker* or *delinquent*. Many teens are very smart, perceptive, insightful, funny, and compassionate, with so many different voices to share—voices that are worthy of being heard by people of all ages, and especially other teens. What do you love about the world? What would you change? You may not be old enough to vote yet, but that doesn't mean your opinion doesn't matter.

But, before we make the mistake of covering your eyes with rose-colored blindfolds, let us make one confession—publishing can also be utterly terrifying. You're putting yourself out there for all to see, an inherently risky but courageous endeavor. Sharing your writing can be intensely personal and extremely public at the same time, which to many people would be no different from that nightmare everyone has about walking naked down a busy street in New York City. (What, you've never had that one? Not fair!) Before you start hyperventilating and toss this book into your fireplace, here's a reassuring thought: You can publish anonymously if you want. And, another: Your work might be really good, and this could be the best risk you ever take. Years from now, you'll pull those dusty old issues out of a box in your closet and smile at the memory of receiving those acceptance letters. So *carpe diem*, people! Adventure awaits.

CHAPTER 1:
THE WRITING CRAFT

· ·

We all know that writing comes in many different forms: stories, essays, research papers, poetry, news writing—heck, even textbooks. We certainly can't claim to be experts on all the various types of writing that you could potentially pursue. Nevertheless, we'll share what we've learned along the way, and point you to some other resources for more detail.

THE WRITER'S TOOLBOX

Every writer has a different idea of the perfect environment and materials needed for writing. The key is to develop an awareness of your own creative needs. First, it's important for you to be comfortable so you can concentrate. Some writers work at home. Others prefer the peace and quiet offered by a library or bookstore. Maybe a café or a park would be more to your liking. Try different locations until you figure out where you feel most inspired.

How do you do your best work? If you prefer to think out loud, buy a tape recorder. Make sure you have it and several tapes at your fingertips when inspiration strikes. If you can't write without absolute silence, get a pair of noise-canceling headphones. Make whatever investments are necessary within reason; they may pay off in bylines later.

We both used spiral notebooks to jot down and refine ideas, and found this very helpful. You can set up one with dividers to organize your thoughts. For example, if you like to compose short stories, poems, and essays, you could create a separate section in your notebook for each type of work. Another option would be to have each section devoted to a different topic that you might like to write about. You may want to get a college-ruled notebook in order to save space. Whatever you do, get a thick one to hold your many ideas. Even if you prefer to do your writing directly on a computer, it's still a good idea to have a pocket-sized, travel-friendly notebook to carry with you everywhere. You never know when that flash of imagination will hit you. Once you get into the editing phase, you will most likely want a good dictionary and a thesaurus, as well.

Finally, if you are serious about publishing your writing, you will need access to a computer and printer. It is most convenient to have a computer at home, equipped with a word-processing program, e-mail, and Internet access. However, you may also find access to a computer at your school, a local library or college, a parent's office, or a friend's house. Nearly all publications expect to receive typed submissions. Additionally, you may find it most efficient, and sometimes even necessary, to conduct your publishing business via e-mail. We recommend setting up a separate e-mail account, or a separate folder within your existing account, for writing-related correspondence.

Also, don't forget to back up your files on a disk or external hard drive regularly.

FINDING INSPIRATION

So, now that you have all the supplies you need, you're ready to start composing your masterpiece. Yet, the blank page of your notebook stares up at you. The cursor on your computer screen blinks expectantly. Help!

We've all faced writer's block at one time or another. (The night before a big paper is due at school, perhaps?) So, how can you find inspiration for your writing? Try these techniques to turn on the proverbial light bulb:

✛ *Observe the world around you.* Because of our often-hectic daily lives, many of us rarely pause to really observe our environment. As a writer, you should pay close attention to the minutiae of life. Often ideas for stories, essays, and especially poems are spurred by a small detail of (human) nature or an event that you witness. Stay alert, and use your senses. For example, have you ever studied how a cat moves? The way her tail twitches ever so slightly, or how her shoulder blades shift fluidly back and forth as she prowls? Depending on how you feel about cats, their silent gait may seem creepy or like poetry in motion, but it's unique in the animal kingdom. Watching people can be even more fascinating. Airports, train stations, outdoor cafés, parks, and doctors' waiting rooms are great places to observe human interaction—or solitude (discreetly, of course). These are places where people from all walks of life venture, and you never know when a funny conversation or an odd behavior going on a couple feet away can spark an idea for a story.

❖ *Look inside yourself.* Record your thoughts and emotions in a journal. Feeling elated at earning an A on a difficult project? Frustrated over an argument you just had with your best friend? Guilty about lashing out at your brother or sister when you were having a rough day? Write it down. You shouldn't feel obligated to write in your journal every day, but be honest with yourself when you do. How do you *really* feel about personal, political, and social issues in your life? How much are your opinions and desires influenced by your parents, your peers, and society as a whole? The more you practice honestly assessing and recording your thoughts, the more insightful and expressive your writing will become. Additionally, if you decide to write an essay or article about an event in your life, such as a unique travel experience, you might even consider quoting directly from your journal. This will bring your thoughts into sharper focus, making the reader feel as if she were really there with you. Such "inside looks" are very desirable in writing.

❖ *Break away from the familiar.* Make a point of taking part in an activity that you've never tried before, even if you feel a little apprehensive about it. Have dinner at a restaurant that serves cuisine you consider exotic or even strange. Strike up a conversation with someone whose background and lifestyle are very different from your own. You may learn something surprising. In college, Danielle joined the South Asian Society and learned a traditional Indian dance for the society's annual performance. This cross-cultural experience prompted her to write an article for the society's newsletter.

❖ *Tap into your hobbies.* Writing in itself is a wonderful hobby, but what else do you really enjoy doing? If you are passionate about playing the violin, consider composing a short story or poem on the topic. Are you a stage manager for school plays? Write an article on what really happens behind the scenes. Because we both enjoy collecting art from other cultures, we once wrote an article for *Skipping Stones* about the history and creation of Russian nesting dolls, the small painted wooden dolls that each open up to reveal another one inside.

❖ *Read!* Invest the time to read a variety of works, from newspaper articles to classic literature, poetry anthologies to pop culture magazines. Perhaps the setting of your favorite novel will inspire you to create an entirely different story. Or, an opinion presented in an article may spur you to compose a counter-argument in a letter to the editor. Reading is how people learn what makes good writing and what doesn't. Of course, you must be careful not to allow your writing to mimic that of someone else too closely. Let your unique personality traits and ideas come through to make your writing your own.

❖ *Research.* Agatha Christie was once asked how she came up with the exotic settings for her mysteries. She responded that she "wrote what she knew." Most of the settings were from experiences she actually had—even if the murders were not. However, writing what you *want* to know may also be an option. The most important thing to realize about your topic is this: Is first-hand experience really required in order to create an informative, accurate piece? If so, you will need to stick with writing what you know (e.g., you probably won't get very far as a romance writer if you've never been in a romantic relationship). If not, extensive research should give you enough knowledge to make your point. This is what journalistic writing is all about. Try your local library, the Internet, or even interview subjects, and then write about your findings. Ultimately, the key is to know enough about your subject—whether through personal experience, research, or both—to be able to write about it credibly. The last thing you want is for your audience to be picking out errors in your article.

Once you have some ideas in mind, grab your notebook and concentrate on getting them out on paper. Don't worry about grammar (yet). Forget about punctuation and spelling (for now). Just pour out those fragments of thoughts, those interesting phrases and details. You might even carry a portable tape recorder to tape interesting observations if you prefer. Be sure to write down or record every unique idea you have, even if you feel immediately that you will never use it. Sometimes ideas may be improved later, or they may lead to new and better ideas. The famous poet Sylvia Plath once said, "The greatest enemy of creativity is self-doubt." Don't let it get in your way!

PROSE, POETRY, AND PUZZLES

As we mentioned before, writing can take shape in many different ways. Some teens prefer writing prose, while others may enjoy putting their thoughts in the form of a poem. Still others feel the need to be creative and develop puzzles or games to provide entertainment for their audience. We discuss these three types of writing below, as they are popular avenues that teens pursue on the road to publication. Please note that there are many other types of writing that will be discussed in more detail later in this book.

Essential Elements of Good Prose

Think about some of your favorite stories and novels. What makes them so entertaining? What aspects of the writing really draw you into the story? Is it a quirky character that you really love? Dialogue that has a special zing to it? Page-turning suspense? Because there are so many genres of fiction—comedies, tragedies, mystery, science fiction, romance, and more—it is difficult, if not impossible, to compile a list of ingredients that every story *must* have. Nonetheless, these elements are found in most successful works of fiction:

❖ *Setting.* Every story should provide some sense of time and place. California in the 1980s. Last summer at your grandmother's house. Mars in 2056. The possibilities are limitless. So, what makes an effective setting for a story? There really aren't any concrete rules; it depends on what type of story you want to tell. Danielle felt that Dan Brown made his best-selling suspense novel *The Da Vinci Code* compelling by using Paris as a backdrop for the tale. In his science fiction novel *Ender's Game*, Orson Scott Card put an intriguing twist on a coming-of-age story by setting it in a futuristic battle school in space. Of course, you should not feel obligated to choose an exotic setting, nor one that even refers to a calendar year or a geographic location. A reader can understand a story about a 20-year-old college student struggling with classes and career options without knowing which state her school is located in, or what year she'll be graduating. By establishing her life stage (young adult) and placing her on a college campus, you orient the reader to the protagonist's surroundings and situation, thereby serving the purpose of a setting. (In the absence of a specific indication of the calendar year or decade, most readers will assume that the story takes place in the present.)

❖ *Conflict.* Nearly every good story is built around some kind of conflict or adversity that the protagonist must overcome. Conflict builds suspense and draws in the reader. The desire to see how it will play out is what usually prompts the reader to turn the page. One excellent example is the very popular *Harry Potter* series of novels by J. K. Rowling. Harry's struggles with his family, the school bully, his teachers, and even his best friends carry the reader through each book—and his overarching conflict with the evil Lord Voldemort compels us to pick up the next novel in the series. Also keep in mind that conflict does not necessarily have to take place between characters; internal conflict can be just as interesting, if not more so. We long to see how the protagonist will overcome her fears and weaknesses, perhaps because deep down, we want ideas on how to face our own.

❖ *Complex, multidimensional characters*. The most fascinating characters are the ones that have several layers to explore. A perfect hero is ultimately boring. Protagonists that have flaws and vulnerabilities, and make mistakes, are much more interesting to readers because we can relate to them. The conflict in a story will do little to engage the reader unless the reader actually *cares* about the characters and perceives that they are truly in danger. If you're completely indifferent to the cookie-cutter heroine hanging off the edge of a cliff, or if you're convinced she's too invincible to possibly fall, you probably won't bother to read the next chapter.

❖ *Humor*. Just about everyone loves to laugh. Why else would long-running television comedies like *Friends* and *Seinfeld* have been so popular? Funny dialogue and amusing characters can go a long way to make a story entertaining. If you can find humor in life's challenges, from the significant to the trivial, it will serve you well in your writing. Obviously, not every tale is meant to be funny. Some are serious, terrifying, or heartbreaking. Still, even these types of stories can benefit from a little bit of humor now and then, to balance out the scary or sad parts of the tale, thereby providing "comic relief." Of course, humor can be very tricky because it is so subjective; what makes you double over with laughter may be unamusing (or worse, offensive) to the next person. But, with practice (or in some cases, a natural gift), you may pull it off.

Of course, there is much more to writing a really great story. Advanced writers can spend hours discussing how to produce believable dialogue or an engaging plot. Check out some of the other resources listed at the back of this book for more advice on writing fiction, or sign up for a writing workshop or camp (see Chapter 3 for more details).

Certain types of nonfiction can benefit from the above elements, as well. An autobiographical piece, such as an essay about a personal experience you've had, is one example. For nonfiction such as opinion pieces or how-to articles, also consider the following:

- *Include personal anecdotes.* Specific examples from your own life experience will not only help to illustrate your point, but will also help forge a connection between you and the reader by revealing your humanity. For instance, if you wind up regretting your overzealous approach to college applications (20 schools, anyone?), share your experience in an article that offers other students advice on what not to do. People are always more likely to listen to those who have "been there, done that."

- *Choose an unusual topic, or a unique angle on a familiar topic.* If you are involved in an unusual or particularly exciting hobby, such as snowboarding or playing guitar in your own garage band, you could write a how-to article to help readers get involved. Or, let's say you want to compose an opinion piece on the contemporary high school prom experience. Instead of writing solely about the present, spice up your article by comparing and contrasting your own prom to stories your parents have told you about theirs. (Include photos, too—clothes and hairstyles from past decades are always entertaining.)

❖ *Use your age to your advantage.* Don't think of your age as a handicap in the business of writing and publishing. Seek topics that you, as a teenager, are uniquely qualified to discuss: from high school social dynamics, to managing part-time jobs.

One final note: Whenever you are writing any type of prose intended for publication, always ask yourself, "What's in it for the reader?" You must objectively consider whether your intended audience will be interested in reading what you have written. Have you ever recounted a funny incident to your friends and had one of those "I guess you had to be there" moments? This is the sort of thing you want to avoid when writing for publication. Will readers really be entertained or informed? Will your work have meaning to them, or is it only meaningful to you? Understandably, this is not always an easy question for you to answer for yourself, so it may help to get an objective critique of your work before submitting it for publication (more on that in Chapter 3).

Lessons Learned About Poetry

In some ways, writing poetry can be much more challenging than writing prose. To begin with, you generally have far fewer words with which to make an impact on the reader. As a result, you need deft word choice and creative imagery to send the right message. Really good poetry is often abstract and subtle, leaving the poem's true meaning up to the reader's interpretation. Techniques of rhyme and rhythm also can be very difficult to master.

Neither of us can claim to be an expert on poetry, by any means. Whole books have been written on the subject. However, we can offer a little bit of advice (based mostly on our own shortcomings as poets!):

❖ *Avoid clichéd rhyme schemes.* Words like *true*, *blue*, and *too* have been paired together so many times that they are all but guaranteed to make an editor roll her eyes. Rhyming poems can easily come out sounding juvenile or gimmicky, which is particularly incongruous when you are trying to convey a serious message. Unless you have an expansive vocabulary and a knack for inventing unique rhyming pairs, you may be better off sticking to nonrhyming poetic structures for serious poems. For humorous poems, witty rhymes may actually enhance the effect.

❖ *Avoid "broken prose" as poetry.* Prose broken into a short line structure is not poetry. Take for example this excerpt from a "poem" Danielle wrote at the age of 13, about a lioness hunting a gazelle:

In seconds
The lioness caught up with him
Sprang halfway onto his back
Sank her teeth
Into his throat
Dragged him down
To the ground.

This straightforward account is choppy and unimaginative—basically a sentence with odd line breaks. It actually seems much more natural when written as prose: "In seconds, the lioness caught up with him, sprang halfway onto his back, sank her teeth into his throat, and dragged him down to the ground." True poetry usually describes an event or feeling through metaphors and other imagery, rather than a literal account.

❖ *Read your poem out loud.* To catch yourself in the act of using clichéd rhymes or broken prose, read your poem out loud to yourself. If the rhyme is cheesy or the rhythm is off, you'll most likely hear it before you'll see it.

❖ *Edit mercilessly, then set it aside.* After ignoring your poem for a couple of days or even weeks, you'll likely find yourself looking at it with fresh eyes when you pick it up again, and may see it from a new perspective.

Creating Puzzles for Publication

Just as earning a black belt in tae kwon do requires many hours of training, becoming a master wordsmith takes practice. One way to stretch those brain muscles, so to speak, is to create puzzles and word games, especially if you enjoy being creative. We've had as much fun making puzzles as solving them.

Several magazines for preteens and teens, including *Creative Kids* and *Skipping Stones,* accept puzzles and word games for publication in addition to stories, poems, essays, and book reviews. In fact, puzzles may very well be the fastest route to your first byline, because editors typically receive fewer of them than poems and short stories. Plus, they usually don't take up much space in a magazine, and they can be made to fit just about any theme. Think of it as a way to get your foot in the door of a highly selective publication.

Figure 1. Example of a word-and-picture puzzle

If you have never made puzzles before, you may want to start with word searches and crosswords. They are not too difficult to create, making them very good for practice and expansion of your vocabulary. Another fun type of puzzle is a word-and-picture game. There seems to be no consensus on exactly what to call these things (one common name is "word plexer"), but they are very popular. See Figure 1 for an example.

The solution to the puzzle in Figure 1 is "flat tire." This was a simple example, but we have certainly seen much tougher ones. You can make plexers using only words, or a mix of words and pictures. If you do use just words, try to use very few and be sure that the size, shape, and/or position of the words have an effect on the solution as they did in Figure 1. For example, form a circle by writing " 4 tune" over and over, thus depicting "wheel of fortune." If you plan to submit such puzzles to a magazine, be sure to send a collection of 5 or 10 on a page as one submission. They are too small to be submitted individually.

There are many more types of puzzles, word games, and riddles that you can submit for publication. Almost anything goes, so be creative! Creating word games is one way to expand your vocabulary, play with synonyms and homophones, and celebrate your love of language.

EDITING TECHNIQUES TO IMPROVE YOUR WRITING

Now that your ideas are on paper, it's time to get a little more particular. Whether you prefer to write prose or poetry, it is important to take time to edit your work. For example, when writing prose, each individual idea or point may make sense, but they may not flow together as a whole. Rearrange your ideas until you are satisfied with your work. Elaborate. Get everything worded just as you want it, and then add a few transitional phrases to connect the pieces and make them flow together.

If you are writing a story, essay, or news article, check the first two sentences. If they are creative and intriguing, you have a good opening that will hook the reader and encourage him or her to continue. If not, you have a weak opening and should change it. For stories, one way to grab the reader's attention from the very beginning is to throw him right into the action, like a movie that opens with a chase scene. Alternatively, you might begin with a funny or enigmatic line of dialogue.

At this point, if your manuscript is still in the handwritten stage, you should type it on a computer and print a clean copy. Have others read and critique it, including people from your target audience. If you have a mentor, ask him or her for feedback, as well (see Chapter 3 for advice on finding a mentor). If your critics' suggestions sound logical and reasonable to you (i.e., if they sound like good ideas), follow them. If not, follow your own instincts. The most important thing is to have confidence in your work.

When you are satisfied with the content and overall structure, it is time to tweak your word choice and sentence structure, as well as correct grammar, spelling, and punctuation errors. Consider using ratiocination. Defined as "a reasoned train of thought," the term *ratiocination* also refers to an editing technique best used for prose. By using different colors and symbols to highlight certain elements of your manuscript, you can catch redundancies in your writing. For instance, have you ever listened to a speech in which the speaker frequently used distracting filler words or phrases such as "you know"? Or, used too many long sentences or passive verbs, making the speech seem long-winded or stagnant? Similar problems can occur in your writing, and ratiocination can help you to see them.

The first step is to check your sentence length. One way to do this is to underline every other sentence in alternating colors, which makes differences in sentence lengths more visually obvious. You can then edit your work to achieve a balance between the numbers of long and short sentences. When all of your sentences are short, the story doesn't flow well. If you make them all long, the story seems to go on endlessly and can be difficult to follow. The main goal is to avoid distracting your readers with lots of very short or excessively long sentences, so that they can focus on the content of your story instead.

Next, take a close look at the first word of every sentence in your manuscript. You might circle these words with a marker to help you see patterns more easily. Check to see if you have started any sentences with the same word more than once on each page. For example, if you used the word *she* to begin six sentences on the same page, try to cut that number in half when you edit. This will give your story more variety.

At this point, you may wish to make changes to your manuscript and print a clean, corrected copy. When you try to perform every step of ratiocination on a single draft, it quickly becomes difficult to read.

Next, circle all of your passive "to be" verbs, such as *am*, *was*, *were*, and so on. "To be" verbs can be very important to a sentence, but they become boring when overused. Therefore, it is best to keep them to a minimum and use more active verbs instead. For example, instead of "I am afraid of her," try, "She scares me." Try to cut your usage of passive verbs in half.

You may also want to mark common words like *get*, *got*, *very*, *real*, *a lot*, *good*, *bad*, *nice*, and *great*. Like passive verbs, these words are overused and not very descriptive, so try to replace them with more specific terms. Take the word *bad*, for example. Instead of *bad apple*, *bad play*, or *bad boy*, try *rotten apple*, *boring play*, or *mischievous boy*.

Finally, you should give your work an overall proofreading. Verify your grammar and punctuation. As for spelling, if you are using a word processing program, don't rely entirely on the spell checker function. If you accidentally print the word *their*, for example, when you meant *there*, the spell checker won't catch the error, as both words are spelled correctly. If you prefer to print out your work and edit by hand, you may wish to use the following proofreading marks:

^	Add a letter, word, phrase, sentence, etc.
⌄	Add a comma.
⌄	Add a period.
/	Change to lowercase.
≡	Change to uppercase (capital).

└─ Start over here with a new paragraph; indent.

⌒ Switch letters, words, or punctuation marks.

˅̬ Add quotation marks.

_ℊ Delete a letter, word, phrase, sentence, paragraph, or punctuation mark.

Figure 2 shows an example of a paragraph edited with proofreading marks.

Keep in mind that ratiocination and the proofreading marks are just tools you can use to help with the editing process. As you continue to evolve as a writer and improve your editing skills, you may develop your own techniques.

One caveat is that you are not always bound by the rules of English grammar, depending on the nature of your material. For example, some writers will create stories in a "stream of consciousness" style, with lots of sentence fragments, to imitate human thought. (People do not generally think in complete sentences.) The same may be said of poetry, which is in many ways a much freer form of expression. The poet e. e. cummings, for example, is known for ignoring the rules of capitalization in his poems and even in his own name. However, formal nonfiction (such as news articles) virtually always require correct grammar, except for the occasional sentence fragment used for emphasis. You may have more leeway with casual, conversational nonfiction. And, for writing of any form, make sure your spelling is correct unless a deliberately misspelled word serves a special purpose in your piece.

suddenly

Lost and frustrated, I reached a dead end. In the darkness, I could barely make out the gravel-covered area just off the road to my left, but at least I could tell there was room for me to turn around there. Fine, that'll work. I figured, but a few seconds later, when I stopped moving and could get only my wheels to spin as I pressed on the gas, I decided it wasn't working at all. Stepping out of the car to investigate, I scowled at my front wheels, which were stuck about 3 inches deep in mud. My first attempt at self-rescue involved pulling the car from behind. Of course, that didn't work, especially since I forgot to put the gearshift in neutral.

Figure 2. Paragraph edited with proofreading marks

CHAPTER 2:
FREELANCE PUBLISHING

· ·

SELECTING YOUR TARGETS

You've decided to pursue the title of "published author." If you're anything like we were when we started, you're eager to get the address of your favorite magazine, write something, stuff it in an envelope, send it off, and wait for a glowing acceptance letter. However, publishing does have at least one thing in common with playing pool: You must consider carefully what you are aiming for before you make your move.

First, take a look at the market directory in the back of this book (see Chapter 5). A *market* is any newspaper, magazine, Web site, or book publisher that accepts the work of *freelance writers*—independent writers who are not on the staff of the publication. It can also include writing contests. We have listed some important information about each publication, such as types of works published and tips from the editors to increase your chances of success. Resources at your local library may also be available to help you find local outlets for your work.

For example, many newspapers accept work from freelance writers for sections such as travel, arts and entertainment, and lifestyle. Some even have special sections devoted to kids and teens. Search online as well—the Internet contains a vast array of online publications, as well as Web sites associated with print publications and contests.

Create a list of the markets that appeal to you. Make sure that you are within the required age group for contributors (if any), and that the market's other characteristics meet your needs. For example, you may be unwilling to wait a year for publication, preferring to see your work in print within a few weeks or months after acceptance. This will limit your choices, because quite a few markets have long *lead times*, or the period of time between the acceptance and the publication of a manuscript. Perhaps you only write poems and therefore wish to stick to literary journals, or maybe you are picky about length limits. You might even insist on payment, although we would not recommend this standard because it would severely limit your market choices (few magazines pay for student writing, though there are exceptions). However, most magazines do send complimentary copies or contributor's copies to all writers published in a given issue. If a publication's guidelines don't say that it provides these, it never hurts to ask for a free copy of the issue in which your work appears. Also, be sure to consider copyright agreements and rights (see "Rights and Copyright" section below).

As you are making your market list, set realistic goals. As a novice writer, sending a manuscript to a major mainstream publication like *People* magazine or *Reader's Digest* and expecting to have it published is probably setting yourself up for dis-appointment. Publications like these are very tough markets for teens and adult professional writers alike. Instead, start small and work your way up. Aiming to have three poems pub-lished in your favorite youth magazine is realistic; expecting to write a string of best-selling novels before you are 25 is not.

Once you have chosen some appropriate markets, you need to obtain each publication's *writer's guidelines*. The guidelines will tell you what types of work are welcome, what information needs to be included with each submission, and how to format your manuscript. They may also list themes for upcoming issues, spec-ify length limits, or provide any other information about what the editors want. Many periodicals, even print-only ones, now have Web sites and post their guidelines online. Alternatively, you can request guidelines via e-mail or snail mail, using business let-ter format. The guidelines themselves are free, but if you request them by mail, you should enclose a self-addressed stamped enve-lope (SASE) for the editors to mail the guidelines back to you. If you encounter a market such as a newspaper that does not have a set of prepared guidelines, contact the editorial offices and ask how to go about submitting work for publication.

While guidelines will offer a brief description of the publi-cation and instructions on how to submit, you must also read sample issues of the publication before submitting your work, in order to get a feel for the magazine's audience, content, and style. Editors will not accept work that does not suit their audi-ence, no matter how exceptional the writing may be. Magazine staffs often suggest that you read not just one, but several back issues to learn what their needs are. If you don't subscribe to the magazine yourself, try to locate an issue at the library, ask around at school, or try your local newsstand or bookstore. In many cases you can order a few sample copies from the publication itself. However you go about it, try to find as many back issues as you can and study them thoroughly. Read them from cover to cover, even the sections that don't particularly interest you. Take a look at the ads, if any, to get a sense of their target audience. A magazine's Web site can also be an invaluable source of information, from writer's guidelines to editors' advice, and it may even display sample pages from the latest issue. We cannot stress enough the importance of careful market research. The last thing you want to do is write a poem or story and then send it to every magazine you can think of in a mass mailing, with no regard to their individual requirements. Editors can see through this game, and they find it tremendously annoying.

Bottom line—you will greatly increase your rate of success in freelance publishing if you submit only your best work and choose the market for which it is most ideally suited.

PREPARING YOUR SUBMISSION

Follow the Submission Guidelines

Once you have the guidelines in hand, study them very carefully. You must follow these to the letter. Many editors will automatically reject work that does not follow their guidelines exactly. We don't mean to alarm you; we just want to tell it like it is, because editors are always harping on this. Of special importance, is the inclusion of all requested information and materials, using the desired format. Preparing your submission properly is key to giving the editor a positive first impression of your work. (Seriously, if you were an editor with an avalanche of mail to wade through every day, would you even bother to read a haphazard, dog-eared, or illegible submission? Probably not.) Keep reading for some specific tips on how to format your manuscripts.

When corresponding with publications, we recommend using the editor's name in your greeting unless instructed otherwise. For each market listed in our directory, we have indicated to whom submissions should be addressed. The writer's guidelines will typically state this, as well. In many cases, publications specifically request that submissions be sent to the "Submissions Editor," rather than a particular person. If your target market does not, then it never hurts to find a name (particularly when submitting to a more adult market), because it shows that you've done your homework. Look in the beginning of a sample copy and find the *masthead*, which is simply a list of all the staff members who work for a publication (typically given in fine print). Usually a managing editor or senior editor is the right person to try. If you're not sure of the right name, contact the staff and ask to whom submissions should be addressed.

Before preparing your submission, first check the guidelines to see whether the publication will accept *unsolicited manuscripts*—complete items that the editor did not specifically ask to see. If not, you will first need to write a query letter to the editor, describing your work and asking whether the editor would like to see the complete manuscript. Most youth publications will consider unsolicited manuscripts, so if the guidelines do not specify either way, it's probably safe to assume that a query letter is not required. In that case, you can skip the next section and proceed with your submission.

Preparing a Query Letter

If you *do* need a query letter, include a brief description of the piece (subject, approximate length, where it might fit in the magazine or newspaper, and so on) and ask if the editor would be interested in reading it. Also include a little bit of background information about yourself. Essentially, you want to convey to the editor why your work would be right for her publication, why her readers will want to read it, and what makes you just the right person to write it. (You want to appear confident here, but not arrogant. If you are having trouble striking that balance, find an objective critic to review the query letter for you.) If you have had other work published before, particularly if it is similar in tone or style, you may wish to mention that and include a copy of it. Check the guidelines for any specific instructions regarding query letters.

You can write a query letter even if you simply have an idea for a story. Some authors prefer not to write a piece until they have found an editor who has shown interest in considering it for publication. Just make sure that you have a focused, refined idea of the topic before you compose your query. If you have already written the piece, it may help to include a brief excerpt of it with your query letter to give the editor a taste. Above all, your query letter should demonstrate both your writing style and your solid grasp of grammar, so proofread it carefully. Finally, don't forget to include all of your contact information (name, address, phone number, and e-mail) so that the editor can get back to you. Send your query in a standard No. 10 business envelope (4.125" by 9.5") with a SASE for reply, or via e-mail (depending on the publication's guidelines).

Figure 3 is an actual query letter that we sent to *Blue Jean* (a national magazine for teen girls that, sadly, is no longer in business). We have modified the letter somewhat to improve it further, but the original did receive a positive response, resulting in the proposed article being published.

Writing a Cover Letter

When you are ready to submit a full manuscript, you must enclose a cover letter. In this letter you should introduce yourself, give the title of your work, and briefly summarize it. Again, address the editor by name if possible, and thank him for considering your work. If you are sending the manuscript after receiving a positive reply to a query, state this in your cover letter to remind the editor of his or her request to see it. When submitting work by e-mail (again, only if the publication accepts this type of submission), the cover letter should appear first in the body of the message. Figure 4 is a modified version of a cover letter that Jessica wrote at age 18.

Some magazines may require you to include a statement indicating that your work is original and written by you alone (not plagiarized). Specific instructions will be provided in the writer's guidelines if this is the case.

Jessica Dunn and Danielle Dunn
[Home Address]
August 8, 1996

Blue Jean Magazine
For Teen Girls Who Dare
P.O. Box 90856
Rochester, NY 14609

To the Teen Editorial Board:

We are twins who are almost 16 years old, and we have a nonfiction personal essay topic that we feel might interest you. The two of us have written a book called *Your Name in Print: A Teen's Guide to Getting Published*. In February 1995, it was accepted for publication by Prufrock Press, the same company that publishes *Creative Kids*, a national magazine of student writing. The process of publishing this book has been a magnificent experience for us, and we would like to describe it in an entertaining and informative article for your readers.

Though we wrote our book about 2 years ago, we first began publishing in 1992. Throughout the last 4 years, we've published puzzles, poems, and an article in various magazines in the United States. The book, however, has been by far our most unique and challenging project to date.

Even after acceptance, there was a lot of editing to be done, mostly additions that our editor instructed us to make. We even had the opportunity to visit Prufrock Press's offices in Waco, TX. We now know more about publishing than we did before we wrote the book because our editor had so much advice to share, and because we had the experience of book publishing itself, something we'd never done before. We believe that by sharing our experiences with *Blue Jean*'s readers, we will show them that success is a matter of a little luck, talent, and planning, and lots of perseverance. Better yet, they may learn something about a new hobby that they might like to try. Please let us know if you would be interested in reading an essay on this topic and considering it for publication. We would appreciate any suggestions you may have for us as to how to go about writing the article. Thank you.

Sincerely,
Jessica Dunn
Danielle Dunn

Figure 3. Example of a query letter

Jessica Dunn
[Home address]
July 6, 1999

Skipping Stones
P.O. Box 3939
Eugene, OR 97403-0939

Dear Mr. Toké,

Enclosed is an article I have written about Russian lacquer boxes, which I collect. In case you haven't heard of them, they are miniature decorative boxes handmade and hand painted in Russia with extraordinary detail. The article is about 580 words long and describes what the boxes are, how they are made, etc. I have also enclosed drawings of the lids of three boxes, which were all created freehand by myself based on actual Russian lacquer boxes. Please consider these for publication in *Skipping Stones*.

As you can probably tell from reading the article, I decided to write it just because I love Russian lacquer boxes so much. I have a great deal of interest in other cultures, and love to learn the cultural meaning behind items I collect. The talent that goes into making these boxes is fascinating, and they tell many interesting stories. Best of all, each one is different.

I would love for you to consider my article and the artwork for publication. Thank you.

Sincerely,
Jessica Dunn

Figure 4. Example of a cover letter

Common Rules to Follow for Submissions

Magazines vary in their format requirements for manuscripts, but most of them agree on some universal rules. Chief among them: If you want to make a good impression, it's important to keep things simple and polished. Unless the writer's guidelines say otherwise, we recommend the following for submissions via mail:

❖ Label every page with your name.
❖ Always print a fresh copy of your manuscript and cover letter

on standard, white, unlined computer paper (no stationery). If your manuscript was previously rejected, never send the same copy to a different publication, as it most likely will have been folded, worn, or written upon by the editor.

- ❖ Print your work only on one side of the paper, using a simple style of type (no fancy fonts, just ordinary print such as Arial or Times New Roman).
- ❖ Choose a readable type size—nothing enormous or microscopic. A 10- to 12-point size is usually appropriate depending on the font.
- ❖ Always double-space your work if submitting a hard copy. Poetry may be an exception to this rule.
- ❖ For prose, left-justify your manuscript (all words are lined up at the left margin). (Fully justified is another acceptable type of format where the text aligns to both the left and right margins.)
- ❖ Leave at least a 1-inch margin on all sides of each page.
- ❖ Don't use paper clips, staples, folders, or report covers.
- ❖ Don't hand write on work or make other marks. Go easy on the whiteout.
- ❖ Write neatly on white or brown envelopes. Don't use colors, pictures, stickers, or tape. Basically, don't try to be cute. So as not to fold your manuscript, we recommend 9" x 12" envelopes.

Beyond these suggestions, it depends on the publication. Be sure to follow the submission guidelines. Figure 5 is a sample manuscript format.

When submitting your work by mail, always send a SASE for a response, unless the guidelines specifically say not to. Most youth publications will not respond if you don't send an envelope with postage. (Some publications respond only to accepted material and, therefore, may not require SASEs.) SASEs sent with submissions are ideally midsize, about 6" x 9". This way, they are easy to enclose within your manuscript envelope, yet large enough to accommodate multiple pages if your work is returned.

If you can, get a stamp or labels with your name and address on them. It takes less time than writing your return address on submission envelopes and your address on SASEs. It's also neater for the post office and looks very sharp. (You can order them online at sites such as http://www.currentlabels.com.) Make sure labels are plain white with a simple font.

Postage

Postage stamps can become costly if you make frequent submissions. In order to save yourself some money, it is best to buy not only first-class stamps but some of the cheaper ones, as well. Then you can combine stamps of different prices so that you don't spend any more money than necessary. If you take your submissions to the post office, they will tell you the exact amount of postage needed. We recommend putting enough postage on your SASE to cover the cost of returning your manuscript in case it is returned with the publication's response (although that is not always the case).

A special note about submitting to international markets: Many great contests and periodicals are based outside the U.S.

Danielle Dunn
123 Writers' Lane
City, State 12345
Tel.: 222-555-6789
E-mail: danielle@webmail.com

One Last Adventure

With graduation quickly approaching, I felt that timeless desire of students everywhere: the need for One Last Adventure before entering the workforce. By April, I had a plan. It really wasn't that complicated. Shortly after graduation, I would fly to Dublin, Ireland, with a work visa in hand and stay in a hostel while hunting for a job as a waitress or secretary or store clerk. Upon finding work, I would look for an apartment nearby. Within maybe 2 weeks I would be settled and could spend my weekends traveling around the country. Ten whole weeks on the Emerald Isle. Yes, indeed, it was a beautiful plan.

Four weeks after my plane touched down in Dublin, the job still eluded me. I had scoured the *Evening Herald*, applied within 50 shops and restaurants, and registered with at least six employment agencies, but circumstances were not in my favor. Dublin's university students, already on summer break, had snatched up most of the short-term jobs before I had even left the States. Competition was fierce for the few remaining jobs. I had no experience as a waitress or sales clerk and could only commit to 10 weeks of work in any position—not a very appealing combination to most employers.

Meanwhile, the Four Courts Hostel had become my permanent residence. Sure, it was clean and cheerful with friendly staff, but hostels are definitely not designed for long-term stays. Imagine sharing a dormitory-style room with as many as 11 other people, and a small bathroom with up to 20, for 4 weeks. Soap theft was the least of my problems. I began to reminisce wistfully about my dorm room at school, and home was sounding like Versailles. I did meet a lot of interesting people from all over Europe, but each new acquaintance would depart within a couple of days, bound for Northern Ireland or Scotland or Paris. I couldn't really get to know anyone.

With no job and no apartment to call home, I felt very down on myself and more than a little homesick. What had happened to my One Last Adventure? I refused to waste any more time feeling like a failure when I had tried my best.

| Dunn | "One Last Adventure" | page 2 |

Finally, I made a conscious decision to stop hunting for a job and start living in Ireland. I toured castles and mansions, went horseback riding in Dingle, and stayed at a lovely B&B in Galway. At the Cliffs of Moher in County Clare, I lay down on my stomach and bellied out to the edge to watch the Atlantic Ocean crash against the rocks 650 feet below me. It was a glorious day, and despite all the tourists, this was a remarkably peaceful spot. I looked out in the general direction of home and was delighted to find that I didn't long for it. Instead, I was more grateful than ever to be in Ireland.

Incidentally, one of the employment agencies in Dublin finally found two brief assignments for me, audiotyping for two lawyers and answering the phones at the Irish Food Board. I returned home early (to save money) but far from disappointed. Though not quite the summer I had planned, it definitely qualified as One Last Adventure.

Figure 5. Sample manuscript format

Making submissions to a foreign country will generally require International Reply Coupons (IRCs), which can be purchased at a post office. These must be enclosed with your SASE rather than U.S. postage stamps. The editors will use the IRCs to purchase their own country's postage stamps, which can then be placed on your SASE and mailed. Alternatively, some foreign publishers, particularly those in Canada, may accept U.S. currency as payment for postage. It never hurts to ask. Use U.S. stamps on your outer envelope to submit your work. Be sure to ask the post office how many stamps are needed for your envelope; international mail always costs more.

Submitting Work Via E-mail

For many markets, you can avoid the hassles of envelopes and stamps entirely by submitting your manuscript via e-mail—a very convenient option if the publication accepts online submissions. The medium may seem inherently casual, but don't treat it that way. It's important to be just as professional in electronic communication as you would be by mail. A few tips are listed below:

- Use meaningful subject lines. For example, a subject like "'Help, My Aardvark Has Run Amok!,' a poem by Eureka Squeegee" will help the editor keep track of your message, whereas "Submission" is virtually useless as a label. Just imagine trying to sift through 600 e-mails that all have nothing but "Submission" or "Question" in the subject field, and you'll see what we're talking about.

- In the body of the e-mail, address the editor by name whenever possible (unless told otherwise), just as you would with print publications. Be sure to use the person's title as a courtesy (e.g., Mr., Ms., or Dr.) instead of his or her first name. It is better to be too formal than to assume it is acceptable to address someone informally.

- The body of your message should contain a cover letter. Keep in mind that a busy editor will probably glance at a dauntingly long e-mail and think "I'll save that one for later"—at which point it will likely get lost in her inbox. To avoid this trap, cut to the chase and restrict your introduction to approximately 10 lines, especially if your submission itself is pasted into the body of the message below.

- Use file attachments sparingly, and only if the publication's guidelines allow it. Attachments are notorious for transmitting computer viruses, making recipients wary of them. They also tend to consume a lot of disk space.

Provided your submission does not require special formatting, in most cases you would be wise to copy and paste your text into the body of your message below the cover letter (unless the guidelines state otherwise). If you do send an attachment, format your manuscript within the electronic file as described above in the instructions for hard copy submissions.

❖ Don't type using all caps just because it's easier than using the shift key. Using all caps is the electronic equivalent of shouting and is therefore considered rude. Save it for the obnoxious older sibling who just went to Hawaii without you.

❖ Use the spell checker. If your e-mail system doesn't have one, copy and paste your message into a word processing program and check it there. Typos look just as bad in e-mail as they do on paper.

It's best not to send the same manuscript to more than one market at a time. This practice is known as making *simultaneous submissions*. Publications will often request the right to be the first to publish a piece. If more than one accepts the work, you will be in a bind and may not get published at all. However, do not confuse this with the term *multiple submission*, which means to send more than one manuscript in the same envelope to the same publication. Some editors discourage this, and if they do, it will be written in the guidelines. In general, we would not advise it unless they specifically say it is OK.

Finally, for some types of writing, timing must be considered. If your piece is seasonal—such as a poem about the carefree days of summer, or an article suggesting the best vacation destinations for Spring Break—you will need to submit it well in advance of the relevant season or holiday, especially if your target publication has a long lead time. Check the guidelines and/or the publication's Web site for tips on when to submit seasonal pieces. If they don't specify, contact the editorial staff and ask.

RIGHTS AND COPYRIGHT

If and when your work is accepted for publication, you will be entering into an agreement with the publisher concerning the ownership of the manuscript. As the creator of the work, you own all rights to it until you assign them to someone else—generally the publisher so that the publishing company may print the piece.

Some publications request *one-time rights*, allowing them to print your work once, after which the rights revert back to you. Under this agreement, you can have that work published elsewhere if you wish. A subcategory of one-time rights is *first rights*. This term means that the publication will be the first anywhere in the world to publish the work. Many publications ask for first rights with *reprint rights*, which allow them to use your work again for anthologies or other projects.

Selling reprint rights can be a benefit to authors, as well. A few years after the first edition of this book came out, we wrote an article for *New Moon* about our book publishing experience. The magazine paid us approximately $36 total, plus contributors' copies, which was just fine with us. But, about a year later, we got a check for $275 in the mail, completely out of nowhere. The accompanying letter explained that our article had been reprinted, and that this was our share of the proceeds. (Our contract with *New Moon* had given them the right to sell the piece to another entity for reprinting, as long as they paid us 50% of whatever they received for it.) You'll never guess where it was reprinted: It appeared in a practice booklet for a standardized test in Mississippi. The article was used in one of the reading comprehension sections. Not only did the reprint yield almost eight times as much cash as we got for the original printing, but it also resulted in our work appearing in a place we never imagined we'd see it.

As this example illustrates, whoever owns the rights to a piece can sell it. If a magazine obtains reprint rights from you, it can use those rights itself (e.g., add your work to an anthology) and/or sell those rights to another publisher if it wishes. Depending on the contract, you may or may not be paid an additional amount in the event that your work is reprinted. In our case with *New Moon*, the magazine sold reprint rights to the test publisher, for which it received payment, and then forwarded half of it to us as the contract promised.

Should you grant reprint rights, or not? If your work is a poem, for example, and you're delighted just to see it published once, with no real intentions to submit it elsewhere, then go ahead and relinquish reprint rights. If you wrote an article for which you could potentially earn more money by publishing it multiple times, then you may want to negotiate retaining the reprint rights—unless the contract says that the magazine will pay you extra for any reprinting they do. In that case, go for it.

Other publications take *all rights*, which means that once they accept your work and you sign a contract, they own it permanently. They can then print it as many times as they wish anywhere in the world in any format, and you cannot submit that work to any other publication without their permission. Often, however, youth publications that request all rights will still allow the student to self-publish the work or publish it in a school newspaper. You may wish to ask about this exception.

Rights are a legal issue. Upon accepting your work, editors will most likely send you one or two official forms or contracts to sign. By signing these forms, you grant permission to publish the work, and relinquish the particular rights to your work that are specified in the contract. (If you don't sign the paperwork, the magazine or newspaper can't print your piece.) Your parent or guardian must also sign the form if you are under the age of 18. Be sure to make copies of the completed forms for your files before mailing the originals back to the publisher. Don't worry too much about all of these forms. They are pretty easy to understand, and you can always contact the magazine's editors and ask them questions if you need to.

Once you've done this, the matter is closed, whether the publication uses the piece or not. *Highlights*, for example, takes all rights on accepted works without guarantee of publication. You may want to make sure the piece is definitely going to be printed before signing. If you are dissatisfied with the contract, don't be afraid to attempt a polite negotiation. It never hurts to ask. But, be aware that in some cases, the publication may stand firm on its standard contract, and refuse to publish your piece unless you surrender the rights it has requested. For this reason, it is useful to know up front, before you even submit something, what rights the publication will typically take. If the writer's guidelines do not include this information, contact a member of the editorial staff and ask him or her what rights are taken on published work, and whether the rights are negotiable. That way, you can factor this into your decision as to whether you should submit your piece to them in the first place.

As noted in the section called "Preparing Your Submission," the publication may also require you to sign a statement indicating that your work is original and written by you. This promise of originality may be requested along with your submission or upon acceptance, and protects the editors in the case of plagiarism.

Although rights and copyright are closely related, there are some important issues specific to copyright. *Copyright* is a legal protection against the unauthorized publication of your work. A copyright is automatically placed on a creative work as soon as it is created (as the author or artist, you hold the copyright). Therefore, the work is protected by law against plagiarism. It is illegal for anyone to copy your work or a piece of it without your permission. It is also illegal for someone to claim that your work is his or hers. You can register your work online (http://www.copyright.gov) for a small fee if you like. It's not a requirement in order for your work to be protected, but registering can make it easier for you to make a claim against unauthorized copying of your work.

Copyright becomes very important when your work is published. When this happens, the copyright holder may change. If you have a book published, it will probably be copyrighted and registered at the copyright office in your name by the publisher, and, therefore, you will hold it. However, if your work is published in a magazine, the publication will probably hold the copyright to the actual printed material. This is because publications place (and register) copyrights on their magazines as collective works. Be aware that even if you do retain the copyright of your individual work, the publication still owns the copyright of the issue in which it appeared. Therefore, you may not use their layout, format, or graphics without their permission. You may not use photocopies of the work or any graphic designs they may add without permission, as well.

When it comes to rights, the most important thing to remember is that if you wish to publish a given piece more than once, you need to be sure it's OK with all parties involved. (Please note that many editors are not willing to even look at work that has been published elsewhere, but there may be some instances in which it might be appropriate for you to seek publication in more than one market.) For example, if one of your poems has been printed in *New Moon* and you now wish to submit it to *Skipping Stones*, you would need to verify that your contract with *New Moon* allows this. You would also need to check that *Skipping Stones* is willing to accept previously published work. Because this magazine typically buys first rights, you may want to ask about this up front before submitting the piece. Either way, you should mention in your new cover letter that the work has been published before and where.

You may also encounter the situation of wishing to submit something to a second publication while still awaiting an answer from the first. Magazines with long response times, such as *Teen Voices*, will sometimes allow this. However, before deciding to pursue other markets, it would be prudent to contact the first one to let the editors know your plans and to clarify that publishing your piece elsewhere will not make them less inclined to accept it themselves.

ONLINE PUBLISHING

Up until now, we have focused primarily on how to publish your work in print magazines. However, a lot has changed in cyberspace since we wrote the first edition of this book 10 years ago. Online magazines are more prevalent than ever, and many people create their own personal Web sites. However, there are some major differences between print publications and those on the Internet.

In some aspects, online magazines have the advantage. For one thing, your audience is potentially unlimited. Most American print publications circulate primarily to residents in the U.S. or Canada, whereas online ones can easily reach people all over the world. Indeed, many online venues are international in terms of contributors, as well. Sites such as Kids on the Net (http://kotn.ntu.ac.uk) and Teen World News (http://www.teenworldnews.com) publish writing by kids and teens from any country (although almost everything is in English). If you've always wondered what it's like to be a teenager in another part of the world, this is one way to gain some insight—and you might be amazed by some of the similarities, as well.

Online publishing also may involve much higher levels of interaction between readers and writers than print publishing does. For example, Kids on the Net allows readers to post comments in response to other kids' work. Beyond that, its mission is to promote and expand the concept of "new media writing," which is defined as any type of creative work in which "the computer is an essential component of the writing and without it the work would not exist." One example is a *branching story*, in which the reader chooses which path the story will take at key plot milestones (Sarah's been grounded—will she stay put or try to sneak out of the house?) by clicking on hypertext. Another idea is a *never-ending story*, in which new paragraphs are continually added by anyone who wants to contribute.

Another potential advantage to online publishing is speed. Once each issue of a magazine or newspaper is organized, it must still be typeset, printed, and mailed to all the readers, resulting in delays that don't hamper online magazines. Internet publications may also have continuous turnaround, where changes are made to the site every few days, whereas printed periodicals give you all new material at once and then nothing until the next issue.

However, one of the key disadvantages to online publishing is lack of permanence. When your work is printed on paper, you can obtain a copy of the issue and keep it forever if you want to. By contrast, your piece may only stay online for a limited time. Once it is removed from the site, all tangible evidence of your success disappears. True, you can always print a copy of the Web page, but somehow it just doesn't feel as real. In some ways, the contrast between online and print publication resembles the difference between e-mail and handwritten letters. E-mail is enormously convenient, but its prevalence in our society has made handwritten messages seem that much more special to many people, because of the greater effort required. Some writers feel the same way about print publications as their online cousins multiply. There's also a certain prestige associated with some of the older, well-established print magazines like *Stone Soup*.

You might also find Web sites that feel more like databases than magazines. Many sites that publish work by young writers will post virtually everything they receive, merely screening submissions to check that they have decent grammar and no offensive content. Kidpub (http://www.kidpub.org/kidpub) is one of these, boasting a collection of more than 40,000 stories. By contrast, print publications are often held to a higher standard in both grammar and content due to their limited space and higher cost of production. You may enjoy sending your work to sites like Kidpub, but the sense of accomplishment you get from it will pale in comparison to winning a spot in a more selective publication (printed or online).

That being said, the Internet certainly can provide an outlet for your writing. So, what are your options?

Online Self-Publishing

If you're feeling adventurous and want to have the freedom to decide how your work is presented, you might consider starting your own Web site. You should have no trouble finding books on how to do this. Personal Web sites can offer a terrific creative outlet, in which you would do not only the writing, but also make all the decisions about colors, fonts, graphics, and animation. Be aware, though, that your audience will most likely be limited to family and friends who know your Web address, and the occasional stranger who finds your site listed in a set of search results.

Maintaining your own Web site does require some technical skill. If that's not your cup of tea, try blogging. *Blogging* is the act of creating and maintaining a blog, short for Weblog, which is essentially an online journal. Several free online services such as Blogger.com and LiveJournal.com allow authors to set up their own blogs with remarkable ease, and update them by periodically posting new text and photos. A blog can cover any topic you wish, from a political debate to a hobby that interests you, or a day-by-day account of a personal ordeal with which you are struggling. It can be inspirational and entertaining for your readers, and cathartic for you. The possibilities are literally endless. Most blogs encourage readers to respond, thereby creating a dialogue. You could even create a young writers' club online through blogging, thus opening the floor to your peers all over the country or the world.

But, as with just about any form of communication, blogging carries certain personal and legal risks. Before you go blog-wild, check the warning label:

❖ *Be cautious about security.* Don't share your address, your phone number(s), or other sensitive contact information. The world has its share of lunatics, and the last thing you need is a disturbed reader who won't stop calling you or tries to confront you in person. This advice applies to personal Web sites, as well.

❖ *Know the law as it applies to blogging.* There are rules regarding plagiarism and copyright infringement, libel, and trademarks, to name a few. For instance, if your blog refers to any company by name, you have to be careful not to imply that the company endorses what you write. The Electronic Frontier Foundation (http://www.eff.org) offers a "Legal Guide for Bloggers" that you can access online for free.

✦ *Don't take readers' comments too personally.* Blogging can provide a wonderful opportunity to obtain feedback on your writing, because readers of your blog can post responses. Unfortunately, you may receive unnecessarily harsh words from some who disagree with what you say, or simply feel like being argumentative. Celebrate the positive feedback and concentrate on learning from any *constructive* criticism you receive. Visit an online blogging service to get started.

Online Magazines

Another option (and possibly a less time-consuming one) is to submit your writing to online magazines, which are operated in much the same way as printed ones. You submit your work via e-mail or by pasting it into form fields on the Web page. Depending on the site, your work may be posted automatically, or it may be subjected to a merit-based selection process like that used for most print publications. Either way, your manuscript may be edited for length, content, and grammar. The good news, though, is that it has a much greater chance of being read widely if posted on a commercial Web site as opposed to your own.

The variety among online publications rivals, or may even surpass, the diversity enjoyed by their printed counterparts. You will find everything from literary writing, to entertainment news and gossip, to serious debate about current events—all written by kids and teens. Several online publications are listed in the directory at the back of this book. To find others, try using an Internet search engine to search for keywords like "teen writing online" or "young writers online." Be aware, however, that online magazines may be more ephemeral than print publications. The vast majority of Web sites that publish student writing do not charge readers for access—which means very little, if any, funding for maintaining the site. As a result, the administrators of online publications are often students or teachers who do it in their spare time for no pay. If they run out of time for it and can't find anyone willing to take over, then the site gets dissolved.

Many print publications have supplementary Web components. For some, the Web site may contain little more than contact information, writer's guidelines, and links. Others may post excerpts from their latest issue and/or offer different work altogether. If your work is accepted by *Teen Ink*, for instance, it may appear online, in print, or both at the editors' discretion. Before the advent of the Internet, print publications were invariably forced to turn down some excellent work due to space limitations; cyberspace now provides the perfect means for editors to display deserving submissions that couldn't quite fit into the magazine. Even if you have little interest in online publication and prefer to focus on printed outlets, don't miss the opportunity to learn more about potential markets via their Web sites. Additionally, you may find that the Web sites of your favorite print publications contain links to online publishing sites.

TRACKING YOUR PROGRESS

Believe it or not, keeping good records of your submissions is one of the most important factors in the writing business, especially if you submit a lot of pieces to many different publications. Many effective record-keeping systems exist. You must be certain to choose one that makes sense to you and that you can and will easily keep up with. Below are a few suggestions.

✧ *Ledger system.* Jessica's method was to keep a chronological record of submissions in a ledger with lined pages and columns. She labeled the columns on each page with date sent, title of manuscript, name of publication, the earliest date that a reply could be expected, the date that it actually arrived, and whether the manuscript was accepted or rejected. If you tend to submit frequently to a small number of markets, you could modify this system by designating several pages for each market, rather than listing the publication title for every submission. Also designate a separate column to make note of what rights, if any, you have retained on each accepted piece. This will help you determine which manuscripts you can submit to other publications (although, once again, please note that most editors would prefer that you submit work that has not been published previously). Finally, for tax purposes (and bragging rights) make sure to keep track of any money you earn through publishing, especially if it begins to approach a substantial amount (more than a couple hundred dollars a year). If you prefer to keep records electronically, a very similar system could be arranged in a database or spreadsheet.

- ❖ *Index cards*. Danielle's system of record keeping involved index cards. She gave each submitted piece its own card and included much of the same information that Jessica recorded in her ledger. She kept her cards in a small file box in alphabetical order by title of work. Alternatively, you could tack your index cards onto a bulletin board.

- ❖ *File system*. Consider traditional filing. Label each file folder with the title of one of your pieces and fill it with submission information about that piece, plus a copy of the manuscript if you wish. Then put the folders in a large file box or file cabinet.

- ❖ *Computer files*. If you keep your work stored on a computer disk or hard drive (a very good idea), you may also find it beneficial to save your files by the name of the manuscript. It is much easier to locate your most recent story if the document is saved under the story's title instead of just "Story #24." Don't forget to back up your files—both your manuscripts and any databases—regularly onto a disc or portable hard drive, and keep printed copies as backups, too.

"OK," you might be thinking. "That's all fine for the manuscripts themselves, but what do I do with the rest of my submission stuff?" It's true that you may soon be swamped with returned SASEs, rejected copies of your manuscripts, acceptance and rejection letters, and writer's guidelines. So what should you do with these?

If any of your correspondence comes back "Return to Sender," be sure to make note of that before discarding the envelope. You could discard or recycle rejected copies of your manuscripts, as well, but they may be worth keeping if the editor wrote revision suggestions on them. You should definitely keep your response letters, especially the acceptance letters. That way, you can mail copies of them to your grandparents or other proud relatives or show them to your friends to prove that you really are having your work published. Also, if you wait for more than a year to see your work in print and fear that the editor misplaced it, you can resubmit the manuscript along with a copy of the letter as proof of acceptance. Sometimes when an editor is replaced, the new editor may be unsure of the status of unpublished work sitting in the office. Keep your rejection letters, too. Most published authors proudly display their "reject file." It's a testament to how much work you've done. Response letters could be kept in your files for each manuscript, or compiled together in chronological order.

For your submission guidelines, perhaps the most handy storage method is to hole-punch them and compile them all into one large binder. You can make them easy to sort through by putting them in alphabetical order or by using dividers to separate them into categories of your choice. Whenever you receive a new set of guidelines from a publication, record the date so you can keep track of how current the guidelines are. Be sure to download or request updated guidelines at least annually.

You may also want to designate a desk drawer or file box to house all of your guidelines, records, works-in-progress, and supplies. Do whatever works for you.

One advantage of staying organized is that it enables you to capitalize on improvements in your writing technique by rediscovering and rejuvenating old manuscripts. You can look back in your files and edit your unpublished works (or published ones that you still have rights to). Who knows? You just might gain an acceptance on a manuscript you wrote a few years ago, which might have been lost forever if you hadn't kept such well-organized records.

Some manuscripts, such as nonfiction articles, also can be revised specifically to suit the content or tone of several different publications, allowing you to draw upon the same basic information to publish multiple similar pieces. For example, Danielle once wrote a news article for a local newspaper about a standardized test for Texas students, and how it was driving changes to the state curricula. Using the background information she had gathered for that article, she could write an opinion piece about the impact of those changes on her school from a student's perspective. A personal essay about your family's trip to the Grand Canyon could morph into a cautionary tale about the hazards of taking a road trip with your little brother, or with some additional research, an article about how tourism has evolved in Arizona. This is a wonderful way to make the most of your efforts to research and write an article—and another excellent reason to maintain well-kept records of your past writings and submissions.

Consider keeping a portfolio to keep track of your accomplishments and your progress as a writer. A *portfolio* is a self-assembled collection of creative works by one author. It may include clippings of your published pieces, as well as unpublished work. Using this, you can celebrate your successes and marvel at your improvements—a great resource for staying motivated, especially in the face of recent rejection. Keep the pieces in chronological order by date created; you might use a folder, binder, or scrapbook. This way you may open your portfolio 20 years from now and read it like a book from beginning to end, seeing your writing improve right before your eyes. Portfolios can also be used by professional writers as a form of resume—for instance, as a demonstration of publishing experience when applying for an editorial or writing position.

In addition to keeping a portfolio (or perhaps as part of the portfolio), you may wish to keep a journal to describe your progress in writing and publishing. Reflect on how you've handled the challenges and excitement of the publishing process. As we wrote the first edition of this book, we both created journals and combined them with letters to and from our editors and copies of the manuscript at each stage of revision. Now, almost 10 years later, we both enjoy these vivid depictions of our experience.

THE UNFORTUNATE REALITIES
OF FREELANCING

By now, you are probably wondering what happens *after* you finally get that manuscript out there, whether via mail or e-mail. As days, weeks, even months pass with no reply to your submission, you may start to speculate: "Was it lost in the mail? Did my e-mail get inadvertently deleted? Are the editors having some raging debate over it? *What's taking so long?*" Try not to get discouraged. Lots of publications have to tackle hundreds or thousands of submissions with a small staff, so responses often take months. You should always wait at least a couple of weeks past the market's typical response time (or, in the absence of that information, 2 or 3 months) before sending a follow-up letter. Don't call about the status of your work even if a response is overdue. We know it's frustrating, but editors are very busy people. If you call an editor about a manuscript, he will probably have to keep you on hold for a minute or two and go dig for it. This can be very inconvenient for both of you, especially if your call is long distance. Send inquiries on the status of manuscripts through the mail or e-mail instead.

Waiting is involved not only in responses to submissions but also in the lead time, which is the time between acceptance and the actual publication of your work. Should your work be accepted, most magazines will send you a free copy of the issue in which your work appears—but you may not see it for several months or even a year or two, depending on the publication.

However, waiting is not the worst thing a freelance writer encounters. The scariest word of all is *rejection*. One of the magazines that we used to send work to, *Merlyn's Pen*, received 15,000 submissions per year. Not only did that mean waiting around 10 weeks for a reply, but it also meant reduced chances of acceptance. *Merlyn's Pen* published no more than 150 manuscripts per year. That left thousands that didn't make the cut.

Regardless of your age, rejection is likely to plague your writing and publishing ventures. *Look Homeward Angel* by Thomas Wolfe was rejected more than 30 times. However, when it was finally published, it sold hundreds of thousands of copies! Even our own submissions can be used as an example. Between the two of us, we made probably 100 submissions before the first edition of this book was published, and had only 20 or so acceptances to show for it. But, we kept trying.

Especially in the beginning, rejection often comes more frequently than acceptance. No writer is immune to it, even if she is fortunate enough to have her first submitted work accepted for publication. We don't say this to discourage you; it just comes with the territory. Some young writers, upon receiving their first rejection slip, deem themselves failures and give up making submissions. This is a big mistake. If every writer on Earth did that, there would be no published authors. In fact, many professional authors are ironically proud of a thick rejection file, because it reflects the magnitude of their efforts and experience.

Never assume that you have failed because a magazine turned down your work. An editor's rejection of your work does *not* mean he or she is rejecting you, and it doesn't mean you're a poor writer. Rejection can result from any number of reasons. Perhaps your work did not quite fit the style, subject matter, or audience age of the publication you sent it to. Or, maybe you submitted a fiction piece, but the editor only needed nonfiction at the time. Maybe the editors just accepted some similar work, or have an extensive *backlog*—a large collection of accepted manuscripts waiting to be published. Also, an editor's decision is based partially on his or her personal tastes; a different editor may have reached a different conclusion. Never think "I'm not good enough" or "I'm a failure." In fact, you should congratulate yourself for mustering the courage to submit your work in the first place.

Also, never assume that just because an editor rejected one of your manuscripts, he or she will reject the next one. Perseverance pays off, so keep sending in your submissions. It may look like the odds are against you, but if you have faith in your talents, and you have researched the publication's needs and studied its guidelines, it's always worth a shot. If you don't have confidence in the ability of your work to be accepted at a particular magazine, either edit until you do, or pick a publication that you think will like your work better.

Sometimes an editor might reject your work but still offer suggestions on how to improve it. It may not always feel like it, but this kind of constructive criticism is actually a compliment—after all, editors are not obligated to do this at all. If they do take the time, it often means they think the manuscript has potential. It would be a serious mistake for you to completely disregard an editor's advice or any suggestions for manuscript revisions. Consider making the changes and resubmitting the manuscript to the same publication or elsewhere. Danielle once received a personalized rejection letter for one of her puzzles from a Canadian magazine called *In2Print*. Because most magazines send a form letter to all authors whose work is turned down, Danielle considered this letter from the editor to be a compliment. Even better, it included a suggestion for how to make her work better suited for *In2Print*. Danielle's original puzzle was a word game about famous Hollywood actors, none of whom were Canadian. The editor recommended that she revise the puzzle to focus on Canadian celebrities instead. She did, and upon resubmission, the puzzle was accepted for publication.

In addition to rejection and long periods of waiting, editing your accepted work can be difficult to swallow. If your piece requires extensive changes, you may be asked to revise the work yourself. You should follow any advice the editor may give you regarding grammar, spelling, and punctuation, as well as advice for rewording any awkward phrases or sentences. After all, the editor has most likely received a formal education in grammar and writing, and is more experienced.

However, if the editor suggests content revisions and major changes that you strongly disagree with or wish to modify, you should contact him or her to discuss it. Because correspondence by mail is slow and would not enable you to have an active conversation over the matter, you may want to use e-mail to voice your concerns if the editor has an e-mail address.

In addressing the revisions you disagree with, suggest compromises but stay calm. Being argumentative will get you nowhere. Once you reach an agreement, stick with it. Do the best you can and send the work back in as soon as possible.

More often than not, however, editors will revise accepted work themselves rather than asking you to do it. You may be surprised when you see your work in print. Sometimes published work undergoes content revisions drastic enough that the author can tell at a glance that his or her work was changed. Many young authors are disappointed with the revisions, merely because they wanted their work to be accepted for what it was, not what it could become. Some feel a slight lowering of confidence when they find that their work "wasn't quite good enough" to be published as it was written. A few may even hate the specific changes, feeling that these made the manuscript worse. Don't let revision discourage you, however. It happens to even the best authors. The editor is experienced; he or she makes changes to your piece to make it clearer for the readers, who might then like your work better. Besides, most youth magazine editors make a conscious effort to preserve accepted work. Usually your work will remain as much like its original version as possible. If the piece has been shortened, consider this: The editor may have had to choose between reducing the length and not printing it at all.

PITFALLS OF PUBLISHING

Although rejection, long periods of waiting, and unexpected revisions are inevitable in this business, there are some problems that you can escape entirely. First of all: writing something you'll regret.

Use Discretion

This is not an attempt to censor you, we promise! Just a plea to think before you publish something you may regret later. Writing is a very emotional endeavor, particularly when you are composing an autobiographical poem or a personal essay. Lots of teens use writing to vent their angst about their parents, their siblings, their teachers, or their significant others. Honestly, we are huge advocates of this. We both keep journals and have written literally hundreds of pages over the years, occasionally griping about our own parents, our classmates, our professors, and sometimes even each other. But, would we ever publish these journal entries? Certainly not without careful consideration of how that would affect the people we've written about—and how it could backfire on us.

Even if you don't name names, the right details read by the right person can still give you away. Your family and friends will probably probe your writing to see if any of your characters could be based on them. At the very least, you run the risk of hurting someone's feelings with a few blunt words. If you publish a blatant tirade about one of your teachers, and he or she happens to see it . . . it doesn't take a genius to imagine what the consequences might be. Online publishing in particular poses danger because of its immediacy. Let's say you just had a fight with your girlfriend, and fire off a scathing blog entry in the heat of your anger. Once you've insulted her in cyberspace, you can't really take it back. At least with print publications, the act of submitting something takes a little longer, giving you time to think about it more.

This is not to say that you should avoid writing about the people who impact your life. That would be virtually impossible. On the contrary, they will often inspire your best work. Just think twice before you publish something that could damage your relationships with them.

On a related note, especially when publishing online, please guard your personal information carefully. It's OK to print your e-mail address and your hometown, but don't advertise your full address or phone number to the thousands of strangers who may come across your writing. Common sense? Sure, but we figure it never hurts to mention it again.

Disreputable Publishing Venues

Sadly, the world is full of people who make money from the sale of false promises (e.g., weight loss "miracle pills," match-making scams, or cubic zirconia billed as diamonds), and the publishing industry has its share of them, too. Watch out for the following types of disreputable publishing.

Vanity/Subsidy Publishing

Many writers want to be published more than anything, and some companies have found legal ways to exploit them for profit. Such companies are called subsidy presses, also known as vanity presses. Subsidy book publishing is similar to self-publishing (see Chapter 4) in that you pay to have your work published; however, in the case of subsidy publishing, the layout, design, and production are done for you. Generally, you relinquish the rights to the work and are paid royalties on book sales. *Royalties* are periodic payments made to an author of a published book, generally consisting of a percentage of book sales.

The advertisements for these publishers always sound so wonderful. They talk about printing beautiful books by talented people and describe in detail the production and marketing process that will take place. Then they encourage you to send your work, listing names of other famous authors who did in order to convince you that it's a good idea. What's the catch? You pay top dollar for everything. In advertisements, the subject of cost is generally brushed aside with vague references to "reasonable fees." However, it isn't uncommon for authors to pay thousands of dollars to see their books published by these types of presses. At that rate, they would have to sell a lot of copies to recoup their expenses. The vast majority of these authors never earn a profit on their books. The fees may be more reasonable for subsidy electronic publishing, or e-publishing, because the book is sold in electronic form, rather than by printing hundreds or thousands of hard copies. However, in this case your work may not even be proofread at all, or you may have to pay an additional fee for this service.

Even if you think the costs are worth it, trust us—they're not. When you send in your work, company representatives will probably respond back saying that they loved it, lavishing praise on you as a great author. You may be a very talented writer, but the praise is most often exaggerated and misleading. Subsidy press employees simply say these wonderful things, whether they are true or not, to get your money. It's not an honest appraisal of your work. Furthermore, you most likely will not benefit from professional editing.

Besides, what's the point in having your work published if no one will see it? Despite what they say, the marketing done by these presses is often very poor or nonexistent. Your money covers production costs and profit for the publisher; why would the publisher care about marketing your book if he doesn't need the money from selling it to recover costs? Your book will most likely sit in a warehouse.

There is nothing illegal about subsidy or vanity publishing, but you will probably wind up feeling cheated just the same. Somehow, seeing your work in print feels empty if this is the outcome.

How can you avoid getting scammed by such a publisher? Do your homework. If you encounter a publisher that makes reference to any fees that authors are expected to pay, contact the Better Business Bureau to get an idea of the company's history. Don't be afraid to ask the tough questions. What is the true success rate for their authors, that is, the average number of copies sold? (The fabulous results described in their advertisements probably are not typical for most of their authors.) Check out copies of books they have published; do they look professional? For that matter, can you even find them? Have your parents and/or your family's lawyer look over any publishing agreements before you sign anything. (This is no time to skip the fine print.)

Disreputable Contests

Also beware of contests that require you to send money in order to receive a prize, or insist that you buy a copy of an anthology in order to have your work published in it. Most contests do require an entry fee or judging fee, which are usually small, and are necessary in order to pay the contest judges and cover the prize money. But, once they tell you you've won an award, they should not be soliciting more money from you. Publication of winning manuscripts should be paid for by the sale of the collection or work, not by hitting the contributors up for cash.

When entering a contest, read all notices and letters very carefully. Don't skip the fine print. Jessica once had a problem with this when she won a poetry contest. Although she was not actually required to order a copy of the anthology in order to be published in it, she naturally wanted one. Unfortunately, the anthology cost her $60, and that was a discount price. Despite the expense, most writers do want copies of their published work, and the publisher was counting on them to fork over the cash. After seeing the book, though, Jessica realized that her accomplishment was hardly that at all. Several hundred people had won this contest, and all of the winning poems were crammed together in small font and random order. In fact, it's likely that the great majority of people who bought the book were poets who got published in it. It was very disappointing. Always research a contest carefully before entering.

A general rule of thumb to keep in mind is to be wary of any publication or contest that requires you to pay in order to be published. This does not necessarily indicate a scam—for example, in the case of self-publishing—but it might. Tread carefully.

CHAPTER 3:
GETTING FEEDBACK

GETTING THE MOST FROM FEEDBACK

"There's always room for improvement." "Practice makes perfect." As annoying as these statements may be, they wouldn't be so cliché if there weren't some truth to them. If you want others to appreciate your writing (which, unless it's a journal, is usually the point), then it always helps to get some perspective from other people. Chances are you've been getting feedback from friends and family for years, but if you want to take your writing to the next level, you should consult more objective critics. Finding a mentor or requesting a critique (from a professional or your peers) may be just what you need.

Mentoring and critique services are related, but still very different. A mentor is someone who gets to know you and works with you over a period of time, offering advice and encouragement. He or she might help you with the writing itself, with navigating the publishing world, or both. Your advisor might help you brainstorm topic ideas, review drafts of your work, and guide you toward an appropriate market for the finished piece. In short, he or she is looking at the big picture of your development as a writer.

A critique, on the other hand, is a very focused assessment of a particular manuscript. A mentor may provide useful appraisals, but many others can, as well, including people you've never met. For example, some professional editors offer critique services through which they can objectively evaluate the merits and weaknesses of a writer's work. Alternatively, you might try posting your work online and inviting your peers to give you feedback. The magazine *Cicada*, for instance, offers an online forum called The Slam for this very purpose. Reviews are particularly helpful if you have a piece that is 90% ready for publication, but you are having trouble getting that last 10% just right.

Despite their differences, both mentors and critique services offer something you need: feedback. The ability to give thoughtful, constructive feedback is a tough skill to develop. (Anyone who has ever struggled to explain just why she doesn't get along with a classmate or coworker knows this to be true.) But, graciously accepting feedback is a valuable skill, as well. Many people get so attached to their own perceptions of themselves that they become very upset when faced with a conflicting perspective. ("What do you mean I can't sing? Since I was 5, my whole family has been telling me I have a beautiful voice!" Never mind that the relatives are all tone-deaf.) However, if we allow ourselves to really hear it, feedback can be invaluable. How can you get the most out of it? Consider the following:

❖ *Know what you're looking for.* Let's say you've completed a draft of your latest story. Instead of handing it to someone and simply saying, "Is this good?," ask specific questions related to the goal of the piece: "Is it funny/thoughtful/ convincing enough? Are the metaphors effective? Are the characters unique?" Or, maybe you don't even want comments on the content; you just want to know if everything is spelled right. Be clear about what you need. This will also save time for the person providing the feedback. You may even consider giving copies of your piece to multiple critics and asking each of them to evaluate different aspects of your work.

❖ *Pick a levelheaded judge.* Don't just request feedback from people who love you, because they have major bias. Choose someone whom you trust to offer a truly honest opinion, someone who has nothing to gain from being too nice or too harsh. In many cases, an acquaintance or stranger would make a better choice than a friend.

❖ *Pick a qualified judge.* He or she may be a stranger to you, as we suggested above, but shouldn't be chosen at random. What does it mean for someone to be *qualified* to judge your work? A professional editor would be one example. Comments from an editor of a youth magazine would be particularly helpful, because he or she has inside knowledge of what youth publications are looking for in their submissions. A successful freelance writer or staff writer could also provide very useful suggestions, based on his or her own experiences and lessons learned on the journey into print. Finally, don't discount your target audience. They are, after all, your ultimate critics, the people you want to entertain or inform with your work. In many ways, an editor's job is to figure out what will appeal to the readers, so why not go to them directly?

❖ *Don't get defensive.* If someone gives you feedback that seems completely out of left field, don't argue or get upset. Hear him or her out before responding. (If you, like us, are completely incapable of a poker face, at least try not to interrupt). Ask her to provide specific examples to explain her opinion.

❖ *Decide for yourself whether the feedback has merit.* Especially when the comments are unsolicited, keep your grain of salt on hand. If, after asking for clarification and carefully reflecting on the feedback, you still disagree with it completely, then move on. Ultimately, it is up to you to determine if the feedback is valid—but don't just discard it without honestly asking yourself if it holds any truth. If you do, you might miss out on an amazing opportunity for growth as a writer. Feeling torn? Try asking for a second opinion from someone else; share the feedback with him, and ask him whether he agrees with it. Make sure the second person is as objective as the first. (This usually rules out mom or dad.)

❖ *Above all, don't take it too personally.* Assuming the feedback is from an honest (ideally impartial) source, he or she is not judging you as a person. The goal is to reinforce your strengths and offer suggestions for improvement. If it makes you feel more comfortable, try requesting written feedback, which may be easier to digest than comments made face-to-face.

Hopefully, you've decided it's time to push your trepidation aside and seek some guidance. Where to start? It depends on whether you're looking for a mentor or a critique. In addition, other options such as correspondence programs, writing camps and workshops, and writers' clubs combine characteristics of both.

MENTORS

There are many advantages to working with a mentor:

- *Personal attention.* Most mentors will work with one writer at a time, and will therefore have the potential to get to know you and your writing very well.
- *Broader involvement.* As mentioned above, a mentor can be much more than an editor on retainer. He may help you out with virtually any aspect of writing and/or publishing (e.g., coping with rejection, scoring an internship with your local newspaper, overcoming your paralyzing blinking-cursor-on-a-blank-screen phobia—you know, the essentials).
- *The price is right (i.e., free).* Mentors generally don't charge their protégés anything. However, you would do well to buy your mentor lunch once in a while or offer some other token of appreciation for her time. (One exception to the low-cost perk: correspondence programs in which your guide is a professional editor you've never met; more on this below).

Although there are many advantages to working with a mentor, there is also a potential disadvantage: the erosion of objectivity. As your mentor gets to know you (and hopefully like you), his opinion of you as a person may begin to cloud his evaluation of your talents or progress as a writer. He may hesitate to share honest criticism for fear of hurting your feelings. Obviously, this won't always be the case—the best coaches know the value of remaining objective—but it's something to watch out for.

Finding a good mentor is not automatic. You need someone with knowledge and experience in writing and publishing and someone skilled in imparting her wisdom to others. (As you may have noticed, many brilliant people have no clue how to teach). You'll also want someone you can get along with, whose communication style meshes with yours. Luckily, there are many different places to look. Potential mentors may include your teachers, a friend of the family, one of your parents' coworkers, someone in your community or religious organization, the editor of a small local publication, an English major at a nearby university—you name it. Find a local writer's club, whether you care to join or not, and get in touch with the group's leaders. Ask if anyone in the club might be interested in coaching a young writer. Tell everyone you know that you are looking for a mentor. You never know whose cousin's sister-in-law might be perfect for the job.

Once you have someone in mind, how should you approach that person to request a mentorship? It helps to have a clearly defined picture of what you're hoping to get out of the relationship. What are your goals? You might try making a list of things you want to work on (e.g., writing more suspenseful fiction or finding appropriate markets for your work). What kind of time commitment are you asking for? Do you just need a sounding board for your ideas, or do you want your advisor to read all 10 drafts of your latest piece and help you pick the best elements from each? Perhaps you just want some help getting started in the publishing world and only need the mentorship to last for a couple of months. The word *mentor* has many interpretations—you need to share your own definition up front to make sure you and your potential mentor are on the same page.

As you progress into working with your mentor, you'll want to sort out the details of how to correspond with each other. One option is to communicate primarily by phone and e-mail about specific questions or pieces you've written, and meet in person maybe once a month to talk strategy (the perfect opportunity to buy her lunch or a latte as a thank-you). Be sure to keep your mentor apprised of your progress and especially your successes. The main reward for a mentor is to hear the good news and receive thanks for his contributions to your achievement.

PROFESSIONAL OR PEER CRITIQUE

Advantages to a professional or peer critique include:

❖ *Guaranteed objectivity*. Sometimes the opinion you need most is that of a complete stranger, someone who will judge a particular piece solely on its own merits. A critic will not be influenced by your past work (good or bad), your personality, or anything else about you. Want to know how your work compares to that of adult writers? Don't tell the critic your age. Want to know if your personal essay makes any sense without the half-hour background conversation you had with your mentor before she read it? Try a critic.

❖ *Targeted feedback.* Maybe you have an advisor who offers excellent advice about writing in general, but lacks expertise in a particular area. For example, maybe your mentor is a novelist, but you're in a poetry phase. Find a critic who knows poetry.

❖ *The comfort of anonymity.* When your critic is a complete stranger, his opinion of you as a person is not only irrelevant; it's nonexistent. You can fall on your face with far less embarrassment. Plus, the comments you receive will be written rather than verbal, so you can react to them in private.

In general, there are two different sources of critique: a formal evaluation by a professional editor or other qualified person, or an informal sharing of opinions among peers. Your writing stands to benefit a great deal from both kinds. Either way, be sure to proofread your work carefully before handing it over to your critics, just as you would before submitting it for publication. Your readers will have a much easier time assessing your content and style if they are not distracted by typos and misspelled words.

Professional Critique

For a formal assessment from an editor, we recommend *The Claremont Review.* The editors of this young writers' literary journal based in Canada will assess one story, one short play, or three pages of poetry for $30 Canadian (the cost in U.S. dollars varies with exchange rates). Instructions and a request form can be found on its Web site (http://www.theclaremontreview.ca).

You may find a *Claremont* critique particularly helpful for any literary work that you intend to submit to a similar magazine like *Cicada* or *The Apprentice Writer* (see Chapter 5 for more information on all of these.)

If you'd prefer to receive feedback from an editor without advertising that you are a teen (thereby ensuring that your work would be evaluated like an adult's), many options exist. For example, SouthWest Writers is a nonprofit organization for writers of all ages; you don't have to live in the Southwest U.S. in order to take advantage of what the group has to offer. SouthWest Writers will review just about anything in English—not just stories and poems, but also query letters, books, and book proposals. Prices are $15 and up, depending on the length of the material. Details may be found on the organization's Web site (http://www.southwestwriters.org). The faculty at the University of Wisconsin-Madison also provides a critique service for scribes of all ages—regardless of whether they are associated with the university in any way—for costs that vary but seem reasonable (Jessica was told it would cost $45 to critique five poems).

One word of caution: Critique services for writers are widely available, but not all may be legitimate. Especially because the great majority of the critiques are offered via mail or e-mail (rather than in-person discussion) and understandably require payment up front, a fraudulent provider could easily cash your check and never respond. Therefore, we must emphasize the importance of doing your research before selecting a source of advice. If you would like to look beyond the ones listed here, we suggest asking someone else for a recommendation. Talk to your mentor, local writer's club, a workshop instructor, or other contacts to see if they know of any reputable services that are worth the expense. If word-of-mouth is not helping you, focus on institutions that are most likely to be trustworthy, such as universities or well-established organizations. Above all, remember that no critique service can guarantee a writer's success. If your Internet search engine coughs up Writer's Racket, advertising an evaluation that's "guaranteed to get you published, for just three easy installments of $19.99 each"—look elsewhere.

In order to confirm that the critique services mentioned here are both legitimate and worthwhile, we decided to submit some of our own work for their evaluation. Here's Jessica's account of how she took the plunge with two of her poems—and what she learned in the process:

> When I was 12 and 13 years old, I wrote really bad poetry. Or, maybe *amateurish* would be the more accurate word. The kind where the rhyme structure included *true* and *blue*, *sun* and *run*. By age 14, I decided that poetry was really not my forte and stopped trying to get it published. However, I did continue to occasionally write poems when I was upset and just really needed to wax philosophical on paper. While my poetic style improved tremendously over time, I still didn't know just how good or bad it was. So, when I chose to submit two of my poems for evaluation, by way of research for this book, I secretly looked forward to finding out just how astute or banal my attempts at poetry were.

> That phrase *looked forward* sounds kind of odd in the context of receiving criticism. But, I sincerely meant it, for one reason: I was not emotionally invested in the response.

Deep down, I didn't really care if I was a master poet or not. I was just curious. Most writers seeking an assessment of their work do not have the luxury of such detachment. But, in a way, it's good that I did, because it allowed me to see the merit in whatever feedback I received, without being blinded by hurt feelings—which means that I can objectively judge the value and usefulness of these critique services and pass my thoughts along to you.

According to SouthWest Writers, my skills as a poet are . . . not bad. Their anonymous response, consisting of about 250 words, included a nice balance of praise and constructive criticism. The editor pointed out that I have a tendency to stretch metaphors beyond their limits: In one 18-line poem, I included the words *glass, mirror, crystal, shard, sharp,* and *shatter.* Obviously, that was a little too much. (Not that I was all that surprised by the comment. I'll be the first to confess that I'm a bit of a drama queen.) Regarding the second poem, the editor emphasized the importance of using concrete imagery and declared that my best line in that respect was "self-worth in the basement." (I wasn't in a good mood when I wrote it.) Overall, I found the comments pretty enlightening, though a tad brief. I paid a total of $35 for it, which covered not only the two poems but also a book proposal (more on that in Chapter 4). Though their Web site promises a response within 5 business days for manuscripts no longer than 20 pages, my critique took approximately 3 weeks (including time to mail back and forth).

I sent the same two poems to *The Claremont Review,* as well, and received a 400-word response from one of the editors. Her review addressed my strengths and weaknesses at multiple levels—everything from pointing out clichés, to praising my use of second person, to assessing each poem's overall emotional impact (or lack thereof) on the reader. In short, I thought the critique was remarkably thorough and insightful. I waited approximately 8 weeks for a reply, but I would attribute that mostly to bad timing, as the magazine's offices are shut down for most of the summer. As for the cost, I consider this service an excellent value, especially because the $30 fee included a 1-year subscription to *The Claremont Review* (which by itself is $18). The editor also encouraged me to e-mail her with any further questions I had about her review of my work.

What did I ultimately learn about myself as a poet? That I mostly enjoy stringing cool words together. My two poems hold tons of meaning for me, but are too abstract or vague for the reader to really connect with them. "Recovery," for instance, was about my strategy for coping with a traumatic experience, but I didn't indicate what that experience was. Danielle thought both poems were pretty good, but she had the advantage of already knowing the details of what I was trying to express. This is a perfect example of how a stranger can offer useful feedback that your sister, well meaning as she is, can't.

~ *Jessica*

Peer Critique

As we pointed out earlier, an assessment from a member of your target audience can often be the most useful kind.

Because most teens write for their peers, a peer critique could be just what you need. For instance, if you are writing an article for teens on studying abroad, then you should seek feedback from other teens to make sure the article is appealing and useful to them.

How can you go about getting feedback from your peers on your latest piece before you seek to publish it? You may not have to look any further than your own school. Try asking a couple of students in your English or language arts class if they'd be willing to take a look at your story or poem. If your school has a literary club, ask a few of its members for a critique, too. For an essay or journalistic type of article, ask a member of the school newspaper staff. Another great way to get in-person evaluations of your work is to attend a writing camp or workshop, or to join a writers' club (these options will be discussed later in this chapter). Hopefully, most of your peers will be willing to read your work and provide comments. Offer to return the favor, as well.

If the idea of getting honest feedback face-to-face gives you chills, consider seeking it online instead. Check out The Slam, which is run by the editors of *Cicada* magazine (to find it, visit http://www.cricketmag.com and follow the link). The Slam is a forum specifically designed to allow teens and young adults (ages 14 to 23) to review and comment on each other's poetry and short-short stories (also called *microfiction*). Every 2–3 weeks, the editors select a few pieces from the rather large pool of submissions to the site, and post them for appraisal. Some of the best Slam submissions may even be chosen for publication in *Cicada*. As the Web site points out, " . . . the Slam is not for the faint of heart. We intend to display all criticism—no matter how brutally honest it may be." Fortunately, they don't publish the full names of those whose work is posted for review. They also insist that the feedback be specific, as opposed to simply, "This is a great/awful poem."

If you explore a little further, you are sure to find other examples of bulletin boards and forums like The Slam. Try a keyword string like "teen writing critique" on your favorite Internet search engine, and see what turns up. Currently, *Teen Ink* and Fiction Press both offer online bulletin boards (see http://www.teenink.com and http://www.fictionpress.com, respectively). Unlike The Slam, these two are not selective, meaning they'll post just about anything you send in. Likewise, the commentary you get back may not be as insightful. Clicking through a few of the posts, we saw a lot of responses along the lines of "Great story!" with little constructive detail to back up the observation. Before taking the time to submit something to a forum or bulletin board, check out a few of the appraisals that other writers have received on the site, to get a sense of how useful they will be.

Once you find a site you like, and have your latest opus ready to go, keep in mind the etiquette of cyberspace. You'll get more comments from readers, not to mention more *meaningful* ones, if you proofread your work closely first to eliminate any grammatical errors, and keep it short. That's not to say you can't send in a longer story for review; try breaking it into installments of a few hundred words each to make it more manageable. Alternatively, you could just send in the few paragraphs that you think need the most work. (While the Internet has brought a stunning array of information to our fingertips, it has also fostered short attention spans.) When people do reply with their observations, be sure to thank them for it. They'll want to know that their comments haven't just disappeared into a black hole, never to be read. Feel free to ask for clarification if you don't understand a comment, but most importantly, resist the temptation to fire off a defensive or angry response to anyone's criticism. And, finally, don't forget to read some of the other submissions and offer your own appraisals. Reciprocation keeps forums like these alive.

CORRESPONDENCE PROGRAMS

Another option for seeking feedback is to enroll in a correspondence program, which incorporates some of the best aspects of both mentorships and critique services. As with the latter services, these programs involve communicating via mail or e-mail with a professional writer or editor whom you've never met. But, they are like mentorships in that the instructor would review several of your pieces and observe your progress over several weeks or months. In so doing, your instructor can help you see patterns, strengths, and weaknesses that you may not have realized you had. Keep in mind that these programs may provide more instructor attention, but little or no interaction with your fellow writers.

One example of this approach is *The Claremont Review*'s Mentors in Writing Program, in which writers receive one-on-one instruction and coaching in either poetry or fiction (you have to choose one or the other) from a member of the magazine's staff. The program consists of eight writing exercises, with the mentor offering encouragement, constructive criticism, and suggestions on each assignment and on the writer's skills as a whole. The program lasts for 12 weeks and costs $500 Canadian or $300 U.S., and financial aid is available. See the Web site (http://www.theclaremontreview.ca) for more details.

Another very similar opportunity is The *Merlyn's Pen* Mentors in Writing Program for students in grades 6–12. This one offers instruction in not only fiction and poetry, but also nonfiction (again, you have to choose one of the three). Here, too, the program consists of eight assignments, although writers have the option to spread them out over 12 weeks or 24 weeks. Either way, the tuition fee is approximately $500. They typically accept everyone who applies, but you may be turned down if none of the mentors has room to take on another student right away. Go to the Web site (http://www.merlynspen.org) to read about the program and to learn more about the *Merlyn's Pen* Foundation in general. When we were teenagers, *Merlyn's Pen* was one of the best magazines out there for American teen writers. It has since ceased (or at least suspended) publication, but the Foundation continues to offer services, resources, and support at its excellent Web site.

At this point, having noticed the price tag on these programs, you might be wondering why anyone would pay for one of those when it's possible to find a mentor for free, or a critique service for a fraction of the cost. But, while cost is certainly a factor, there can be some advantages to mentorships by correspondence that make them worth the fee. You get the personal attention and broader involvement that come with face-to-face coaching, without the potential loss of objectivity. Your instructor can offer not only the kind of detailed, specific feedback you'd get from a critique service, but also can assess the bigger picture of your skills, because he or she will read several of your works over time. Because all communication is by mail and e-mail, there are no scheduling conflicts, and the connection is less personal, making constructive criticism easier to swallow.

Keep in mind that these correspondence programs are very structured, and the instructors tend to take the lead. When you approach a teacher or acquaintance for feedback, it's up to you to figure out what you need from her and to ask for it. Some writers may appreciate the flexibility that this situation provides, while others may feel so confused or uncertain about their writing that they don't even know what questions to ask. If you fall into the latter group, a correspondence program may offer both questions and answers. Your mentor in the program can help you discover what's missing from your writing by preparing assignments for you based on his or her assessment of the writing samples you submit with your application. He or she can also identify special strengths in your writing and help you enhance them. It helps, too, that you will be working with someone who has experience with guiding young writers.

Similar to a correspondence program, though usually not quite as personalized, online workshops provide self-paced writing instruction. The University of Wisconsin (UW) in Madison, for example, offers several online workshops on writing and publishing. Topics range from the relatively general, such as how to publish your nonfiction or write better poetry, to specific subjects like character development and dialogue. Each course costs approximately $150 and includes several lessons you can cover at your own pace. You communicate with your instructor via e-mail. There are opportunities to get individual reviews of your work, as well. For those who live in the Madison, WI, area, there are also local classes, a writers' conference, and a writing retreat. Visit the Web site (http://www.dcs.wisc.edu/lsa/writing) for more information on the UW programs. No doubt other colleges and universities offer similar programs, so spend some time exploring.

WRITING CAMPS AND WORKSHOPS

Although writing is a very solitary activity for many, it certainly doesn't have to be. One exciting and social way to enhance your writing skills is to participate in a writers' camp or workshop. From one-day seminars to full summer camps, local classes to national programs, the opportunities are varied and abundant.

Writing workshops offer benefits to writers of any age and level of experience. When you are new to publishing and maybe feeling a little hesitant, a workshop can help you figure out whether you are really ready to publish. After a couple of years of attempting to get your work into print, you may find that you start to get a little bogged down in the submission process. In that case, it may be helpful to get "back to basics"— the writing craft itself. Particularly if you have fallen into a rut and haven't had much recent success in freelancing, it might be a good time to focus on expanding your writing skills.

Writing workshops give you the chance to practice your writing in a focused and supportive environment. You may learn new techniques first-hand from successful authors, as well as collaborate with and learn from your peers. You'll be surrounded by others who have faced the same challenges you have, and who know what it is like to see their latest masterpiece rejected by their favorite magazine. Their encouragement can boost your self-esteem and motivate you to keep trying During longer camps (those lasting a week or more), it is common for students to provide feedback on each other's work and to engage in one-on-one discussions with instructors. Although participants spend a great deal of time writing, recreational activities are usually available, as well. Depending on the location of the camp, you may even get a chance to explore new territory. *Teen Ink*, for example, offers a 2-week summer writing program in London. See the Web site (http://www.teenink.com) for more details.

Of course, these benefits come with a price tag, too. Almost all writing workshops charge some kind of participant fee to cover the costs of running the program. Fees will vary widely depending on the duration and size of the program, the activities involved, and even its reputation. Additional expenses may include transportation to the workshop location, and housing if the program lasts more than a day. Another challenge is that the more advanced summer camps, which draw participants from a broad region or even from around the country, are selective. You will have to apply for admission and may have to send samples of your writing and/or letters of recommendation from your teachers. Fortunately, there are camps out there to suit just about any budget, interest, and skill level. We're sure you'll find that the benefits outweigh the costs involved.

How can you go about finding a workshop or camp that's right for you? One easy place to start is your own school. Many middle schools and high schools offer summer camps focused on creative arts. Ask your guidance counselor and English teacher if they know of any programs available in your school district. Over the years we both participated in several of these types of camps. Usually we were allowed to choose from a variety of fun artistic classes ranging from origami to drawing, as well as writing. In one writing workshop consisting of about 10 students, we took part in a "writers' roulette" exercise, in which one student would write the first few sentences of a short story and then pass it on to the next person to contribute another paragraph, and so on. It was amusing to see how the story would change direction based on the different imaginations of each of the authors involved. Another workshop culminated in the group's production of a short newsletter to be distributed to all camp participants, including those involved in other art classes. Writing camps run by your school or district offer the convenience of being close to home, are typically inexpensive, and most likely will not require you to compete for admission.

If you live near a community college or university, be sure to inquire about programs there, as well. Check the school's Web site or visit the campus. The admissions office or the English or liberal arts departments should be able to point you in the right direction if there are any programs available. Oftentimes, university faculty serve as the instructors—an advantage to you because they are accustomed to teaching and are familiar with the writing talent of college-level students. When we were seniors in high school, our English teacher asked a college professor to critique our research papers and grade them compared to the work of his own students. We appreciated the opportunity to see how our writing would stack up at the college level. A writing workshop at a university can give you this same benefit. If you're concerned that it might feel too much like school, don't worry. The organizers of these programs usually try hard to make them as interactive and fun as possible. As an added bonus, if you've got your eye on attending a particular university after you graduate from high school, participating in a workshop there can give you a sneak peek of life on campus.

A listing of regional and national writing camps and workshops can be found in Appendix A.

WRITERS' CLUBS

Another fun way to turn your writing into a social activity is to join or form a writers' club. Like writers' workshops, clubs provide an opportunity to connect with fellow authors—to commiserate over rejections, celebrate success, support and motivate each other, and provide reviews of each other's work. Hopefully, friendships form along the way.

How are writers' clubs different from camps and workshops? Clubs are usually smaller and less formal. It may be as simple as half a dozen young writers gathering at one of their houses on a monthly basis to swap stories. You may not have the chance to learn from experienced, professional writers this way, but you can certainly learn a lot from your peers. By joining a local club, you can avoid the expense of traveling to a far-away camp and paying tuition, room, and board. You may need to pay dues or otherwise cover the costs of refreshments during meetings, but the cost should be relatively small. Additionally, most clubs are open to all interested participants—no application required! Best of all, you'll get to know your fellow club members and see them on a regular basis.

Some writers' clubs may be very focused on the writing itself; members may spend most of the meeting time reading and critiquing each other's work. In other cases, the club may concentrate more on the publishing aspects, with members offering information about new markets they've just discovered, or discussing the nuances of the submission process.

You may find that an afterschool writers' club has already been established at your school. Check with your counselor or teachers in the English/language arts department. If your neighborhood or community already has a writers' club that is seeking new members, they may place an announcement in one of the local newspapers. You might also find information using an Internet search engine. If you know any adult writers in your neighborhood, ask them whether they know of any local clubs you might join.

Not having any luck finding an existing club? Or, maybe you have found one, but it doesn't really fit your interests?

Form your own! Spend some time thinking about the details first. How large do you want the membership to be? What will be the primary goals for the group? Also consider any costs that might be involved. Then try posting flyers in your school, house of worship, and other community gathering places. You could even ask your English teacher to do some advertising for you by telling her other students about the fledgling club. Then gather the "founding members" together and decide as a group where and when to meet, and what activities should take place at the meetings. If you plan to critique each other's writing, we recommend setting up a system for doing so anonymously. For example, one person could volunteer to collect all pieces to be reviewed, remove any indication of the authors' identities, and distribute anonymous copies to the membership. This may help to alleviate the authors' anxieties and facilitate a more open, honest discussion about each piece.

CHAPTER 4:
BEYOND FREELANCING

• •

Up to this point, we have shared all kinds of thoughts and advice about the standard process of freelance publishing: Create a written work (story, poem, essay, etc.), submit it to a print or online publication, cross everything (fingers, toes, eyes, whatever helps), and wait for an answer. Although freelance writing is a lot of fun and can be hugely rewarding, many avid writers look for less sporadic ways to hone their writing and publishing skills. Some, such as working on school publications, will help you develop skills that can also increase your freelancing success. Others, like book publishing, may become more accessible to you after you've had some experience freelancing for magazines. All bring their own unique satisfaction.

SCHOOL PUBLICATIONS: YEARBOOKS, NEWSPAPERS, AND LITERARY MAGAZINES

Many junior high and high schools publish yearbooks and/or school newspapers with students serving as the writers and editorial staff. Our own high school even offered an annual literary magazine of student writing and artwork. Don't underestimate the value that these outlets can provide for your writing. Many of you may already be participating in these activities. If you are, stick with it, and if you're not, we encourage you to give it a try.

Why? There are so many reasons. For one thing, it's a great way to work on your writing skills and even get feedback from other students. You might compose an article or editorial for the school newspaper and then ask readers for feedback; or write a poem for the literary magazine and use the student body's reaction to gauge how the piece might be received by a wider audience. Another advantage to school publications is that if you join the staff, you often can do more than just writing. Jessica was on the yearbook staff in high school and college, and she relished the opportunity to not only write, but also to choose photographs and design layouts. Who knows? You may discover that your true calling is to be an editor (more on that later in this section). You also get to make your mark on a little piece of history, particularly with yearbooks, because these will be kept and cherished by your classmates for decades.

Of the three types of school publications discussed here, writing for a literary magazine is the most similar to freelancing. You'll reach a smaller audience, but by the same token, the chances of your work being accepted are higher because you are only competing against other students in your school. Being published in a school magazine is therefore a very realistic goal for breaking into print. Another upside (or cause for a heart attack, depending on your viewpoint) is that such a production is very likely to be read by people you know. When we started freelancing, we quickly discovered that many of our classmates had never heard of the magazines we wrote for; most of them seemed to prefer mainstream fashion and celebrity publications rather than *Creative Kids* or *Merlyn's Pen*. Therefore, if you are hoping to be recognized as a great writer by your friends and classmates, you might benefit from publishing your writing in a campus literary production. The same goes for getting involved in other school publications.

Newspaper and yearbook staff members also have access to all kinds of information about news, events, and student issues and concerns, thereby keeping their fingers on the pulse of adolescent life. Imagine the number and variety of creative ideas that these insights could inspire! Staying connected to your world is a key ingredient for writing that readers can relate to. Of course, part of staying connected is talking to lots of people—by which we mean learning to conduct interviews. This is especially true for newspapers, but even yearbooks often require quotes and other input from the student body. For more advice on interviewing, and developing your journalism skills in general, check out the section on writing for local community newspapers—much of the same guidance will apply here, as well.

One challenge specific to yearbooks is that they typically provide very little space for text. A two-page spread may contain only 200 words of *copy* (in this case, a paragraph describing the group or event depicted on the spread) plus captions for all the pictures. This means that every word counts, especially because people may read them repeatedly throughout their lives. Therefore, you want your copy to be as engaging as possible. And, go easy on the slang—the graduates may have no idea what you're talking about when they read it 20 years from now.

The frustration of deadlines and word count limitations is inevitable for the staff of a school publication, but the benefits overwhelm the hectic moments. This could very well be your most accessible source of practice for honing your writing chops—or a way to showcase the talents you've developed through your freelancing.

WRITING A COLUMN

There's nothing quite like the thrill of freelance publishing—breaking into a new market, setting a personal record for the number of publications featuring your work, taking the leap. But, let's face it: Half the reason each acceptance is so gratifying is simply that it ends the anxiety of *not knowing*. Freelancing is all about waiting for *yes* or *no*.

What if you could devote your energy to your latest piece while knowing in advance that the answer will be "We'll work with you"? (We can hear the sighs of relief from miles away.) That's what writing a column in a newspaper or magazine is like. You establish a relationship with the editors, agree on a topic for each installment, fire off a draft, and then negotiate revisions as needed. It's almost like being a staff writer, but with a smaller time commitment.

Not that writing a column is without its challenges—you have regular deadlines and ongoing pressure to come up with new things to say around the same general theme. Plus, so far we've conveniently sidestepped one key question: How do you go about landing such a sweet gig in the first place? You've got to convince some poor hapless editor to put up with you on a regular basis, which your family can probably tell you is no easy task. (Just kidding. Maybe.)

But, never fear, it can be done. Teen World News online is one publication that retains teen correspondents who write articles regularly. Other periodicals may also entertain proposals for columns; you just have to come up with a theme and suggest it. One of the most effective strategies is to initiate a relationship with a publication by submitting work as a freelancer first. If the editors like your style and accept multiple pieces from you, they will eventually begin to associate your name with a warm and fuzzy feeling (or at least optimism that they're about to read something good). It only makes sense that they would be more receptive to column ideas from a familiar contributor than from a total stranger.

On the other hand, this world is shockingly small sometimes, and you might one day have an editor you've never met asking *you* to write a column. That's exactly how we got involved with a fledgling magazine called *Young Entrepreneur*. The editor-in-chief, Bonnie Drew, was a fellow Houstonian and had read an article we wrote for the teen section of the *Houston Chronicle* about the experience of publishing the first edition of this book. So, Ms. Drew sent us a few back issues of *YE* along with a note: "I read your great article in the *Houston Chronicle* . . . We would love to have you do some articles for us! Please give me a call so we can discuss the possibilities if you are interested." (Cue shrieks of surprise and delight.)

Thus began our 18-month foray into column writing with *Young Entrepreneur*. During that time, we wrote 8 articles, each one tailored to fit with the theme of the issue (e.g., holiday businesses, marketing and sales, summer jobs). Each installment centered on the topic of teens writing for publication. Some of the articles came from paraphrasing sections of *Teen's Guide*, such as the "Pitfalls of Publishing," while others like the column on holiday writing were completely original material. As always, our toughest challenge was achieving brevity; with a tight limit of 350 words per piece, we spent hours whittling away at each way-too-long draft, trying to lower the word count without sacrificing too much of the content. (The 17th-century philosopher Blaise Pascal once apologized to a friend: "I have made this letter longer than usual, only because I have not had time to make it shorter." This ironic predicament describes both of us *perfectly*.)

Each article gave us a chance to experiment a little with content and style. Some came purely from our personal experiences with writing and publishing, while others required research. For one installment we interviewed another young writer who had successfully self-published a book about her hometown. A columnist also can ask for questions from the readership, or even go "on assignment" to participate in something specifically to inform his or her writing. Varying the format keeps it fresh, too: Try a story form to show by example, give advice in a bulleted list, print actual interview text, write it as a letter to a third party, and so forth.

During our relationship with *Young Entrepreneur*, we watched the magazine expand from 16 pages to 38, and even received a raise to 35 cents per word. (This was very generous— if we spent 6 hours on a 350-word article, that came out to $10 each per hour. Especially when many magazines don't pay young writers at all, we were very eager to hold onto this job.)

Of course, you can't put a dollar value on the kind of experience you get from being a columnist, so don't hesitate to jump at the chance, even if the pay is zip. You'll get to know your editor, possibly on a first-name basis, and you'll enjoy much greater control over your work. If Ms. Drew wasn't quite happy with one of our columns, she'd outline her revision suggestions and then let us do the rewrite—or sometimes we'd make a convincing case for leaving something the way it was. Having an actual dialogue with an editor, via e-mail and phone calls, is the best part of column writing.

At a loss for column topic ideas? Ask yourself the following questions:

- ❖ What do I like to do (e.g., learn how to play every sport invented, act in school theater productions, teach frogs to do circus tricks)? What do I like to think or talk about (e.g., politics, art, my lifelong campaign to replace school uniforms with pajamas)?

- ❖ Are any of my topic ideas broad enough to write multiple articles around them? (That pajama thing does not have good prospects in this category.)

- ❖ Would a larger audience find the subject engaging, or does it just interest me? (This is probably where the frogs fall short.)

- ❖ Do I have a level of expertise or authority on the subject? (You'd have a hard time selling a proposal for a column on afterschool jobs if you have had no work experience yourself.)

- ❖ Can I locate any markets for which this topic would be a good fit?

That last question is really the toughest because obtaining an answer will require some research. Let's say you want to write a column in *Skipping Stones* about foreign exchange student programs. Yes, that topic fits with the magazine's multicultural purpose, but does it fill a void? If articles on foreign exchange are already being published in every other issue, then a column wouldn't add much value. In addition, each issue of *Skipping Stones* has a different theme. Thinking about all the different aspects of foreign exchange programs (e.g., funding, classes, culture shock, spending holidays away from family), will you be able to create an installment to match each issue's theme? To answer this question, you would want to check the Web site for upcoming themes and also look through several back issues. In fact, a subscription may be in order. If you read a magazine religiously for a year to develop a detailed grasp on its content and style, then you will be better equipped to shape your proposal. You might even look for ways to refer to past articles in your proposal just to show the editor that you do read the publication on a regular basis. Introducing yourself as a loyal reader (and hopefully frequent freelance contributor, as well) will help convince the editor to invest some of his limited space in your column.

Want to get a taste of being a columnist without the time commitment of doing it all by yourself? Many newspapers across the U.S. also house independent news bureaus dedicated to publishing articles that are researched and written by kids and teens. This can be similar to writing a column, except that you would share it with other writers and may be assigned topics instead of or in addition to coming up with them yourself. One example of such a news bureau is Y-Press, a nonprofit organization of 10- to 18-year-olds that produces a weekly column in *The Indianapolis Star*. The young reporters and editors of Y-Press cover everything from local and regional issues, to world events and even travel in the name of research. For example, 11 Y-Press teens attended the 2004 Democratic and Republican national conventions (in Boston and New York City, respectively) and interviewed politicians and activists. Similar organizations include Children's PressLine in New York City, L.A. Youth in Los Angeles, VOX in Atlanta, New Expression in Chicago, and Young D.C. in Washington, DC, to name just a few. If you live in or near a major metropolitan area, there's an excellent chance you can find a similar local outlet. For further discussion on becoming a staff writer for a local paper, see the following section.

WRITING FOR LOCAL NEWSPAPERS

Looking for a fun way to gain journalistic experience, bylines, and maybe a little extra cash? Because they are longer than magazines and are published more frequently, newspapers often have a greater demand for writers to fill their pages, and therefore can offer excellent opportunities for young writers to break into print. This is particularly true for small community newspapers.

During the summer break after her first year of college, Danielle worked as a part-time intern reporter for a local weekly newspaper, the *Fort Bend/Southwest Sun*, in our hometown of Sugar Land, TX.

The newspaper job gave me a marvelous opportunity to write for publication on a fairly regular basis—one article per week on average—earning bylines and a little cash while also learning from the guidance of Trinh, my editor. I would stop by the office weekly to get story assignments from Trinh. She would provide a brief summary of the subject or topic and any related information she might have (such as press releases, etc.). As soon as possible, I would begin doing background research and arranging interviews with appropriate parties, either in person, on the phone, or by e-mail. Armed with notes and quotes from my interviews, and any background information from Trinh or the Internet, I would then write the article. After extensive editing and any necessary follow-ups with interviewees to gather a few final details, I would submit the article to Trinh via e-mail. A week or two later, it would appear in the newspaper! The publisher also paid me $25 to $40 per piece, depending on the length and subject matter of the article. This may sound like a low wage, but given that many youth magazines do not pay their contributors at all, I thought the checks from the *Sun* were a nice bonus.

One of the most appealing aspects of the job was the variety of story assignments. I wrote about local residents—a published mystery writer, a computer prodigy, a collector of Mickey Mouse memorabilia—as well as organizations, from an Asian American counseling center, to a quilting bee. One of the leaders of the quilting bee actually sent me a personal note to thank me for writing the article, because it helped attract new members to her organization. On the other hand, I once got stuck attending a (very boring) city council meeting that ran for 4 hours, only to produce an article about the most interesting item on the agenda: installation of some new speed bumps. The glamour of life as an intern reporter comes and goes.

One of the challenges for me was feeling self-conscious about my age, especially whenever I interviewed someone much older than myself. I kept thinking the person would take one look at me and wonder, "Isn't my story important enough for the newspaper to send a professional to interview me? How come I got stuck with this rookie?" But, over the course of the summer, I learned to give others and myself the benefit of the doubt. I found that most people would regard me as a professional as long as I acted like one. Dressing the part (in a suit, or a nice shirt and slacks) also helped. Being confident and assertive when necessary, progressing in the job, and writing good articles were the keys to earning respect. And, the experience was its own reward.

~ Danielle

There are many advantages to writing for a local newspaper:

- ❖ *Contributing to the community.* Keeping the public informed about local news really is a service to the community.
- ❖ *Relatively short lead times.* You probably will have to wait only a week or two to see each of your articles in print. Sometimes, depending on the assignment, your deadline, and the space the paper has to fill, your article may appear in the paper the day after you give it to the editor, especially at a daily or twice-weekly newspaper.

- ❖ *Flexible hours.* Although some of your interviews may have to be conducted during business hours, for the most part you will have a lot of flexibility as to when you do your research and write your articles.
- ❖ *Learning from the editor's input.* As noted above, the revisions made and advice provided by your editor can help you improve your writing and editing skills.
- ❖ *Increasing responsibility.* Although the editor will most likely assign you story topics in the beginning, he or she may grant you some more autonomy as you gain experience. You may then have the opportunity to pitch your own story ideas.
- ❖ *A taste of journalism.* Even a short stint as a newspaper reporter can give you an idea of whether you might be interested in pursuing journalism as a career.

So, how does one go about finding a position as a reporter or contributing writer for a newspaper? One practical place to start is by obtaining copies of all of the local newspapers in your area. If your family does not subscribe, you can buy a single copy of each newspaper at your local grocery store or newsstand. You probably will have the most success with weekly newspapers that have a relatively small circulation, rather than daily newspapers that serve a large metropolitan area. (Realistically, you will not be writing for the *New York Times* right away.)

Read each newspaper thoroughly, including the articles that you do not personally find interesting. You want to get a sense of the tone and writing style of the newspaper, as well as the subject matter of the various sections. Then, check the fine print. You can usually find the masthead, which provides information about the newspaper's editorial staff members and how to contact them, on the second page of the front section. If you are interested in writing for a particular section, such as sports or entertainment, then contact the section editor. Otherwise, you should address your inquiry to the managing editor.

Send an e-mail or letter to the appropriate editor, asking whether there are any open opportunities to write for the newspaper. Your inquiry should be structured like a query letter (see Chapter 2). Briefly describe any previous writing experience you have had, and explain what types of articles you would like to write for the paper. Let the editor know what you can bring to the job. Remember that he or she will be reading your e-mail or letter closely to check out your writing ability, so be sure to double-check your grammar.

If the editor responds with interest, he or she will probably want to set up an interview with you. Put together a one-page resume detailing your past writing experience and/or work experience (see Figure 6). School yearbook or newspaper staff work and freelance publishing credits are all relevant items to include. You may also wish to list any summer or afterschool jobs you have had, even if they have nothing to do with writing. Any steady work experience at all shows that you are responsible and capable of working with others. If you have written and published any nonfiction articles, you should bring clips with you to the interview to give the editor an idea of your writing style and ability. Offer to send them to the editor in advance via e-mail or mail, as well.

Danielle Dunn
123 Writers Lane
City, State 12345
Phone: 222-555-6789
E-mail: danielle@webmail.com

Objective: To secure a position as a part-time reporter for the *ABC Herald*.

Experience

August 2005–Present: Viking High School Yearbook Staff Member
- Composed copy for the academics and clubs/organizations sections of the yearbook.
- Interviewed fellow students to obtain quotes for the yearbook.
- Served as layout assistant using PageMaker.

Summer 2004: Brown & Smith Law Firm
- Assisted lawyers with typing and filing documents

2003–Present: Freelance Writer
- Published a poem and a short story in *Creative Kids* magazine.
- Created word games for publication in *Merlyn's Pen*.

Computer Skills

Proficient in Microsoft Word, Excel, and PowerPoint
Proficient in Adobe PageMaker
Proficient in the use of e-mail and the Internet

Figure 6. Example of a resume

During the interview, you'll want to send the message that you are interested in the job, willing to put forth the effort required, and above all, flexible. You may not be paid the same amount for each article you write; it will depend on the length and subject matter. The editor may occasionally ask you to report on a topic that does not particularly interest you. If you can take these and other adjustments in stride, you are well on your way to becoming a successful reporter.

If you are having difficulty finding a newspaper that will hire you as a paid reporter, consider offering to write for free. As described above, there are many benefits to newspaper writing beyond getting paid. Alternatively, you may offer to work temporarily as an assistant in the editorial office, or ask if you can "job shadow" one of the reporters to learn more about what they do and how. These options would at least give you a foot in the door, and potentially an opportunity to do some writing later on.

Once you have the job, how does the process of writing for a newspaper actually work? You've heard Danielle's story, but there will be some variation from one newspaper to the next, and even from one editor to the next. However, the following suggestions should prove useful for any type of news article that you may write.

Inevitably, you will need to interview people for your articles. Interviewing is one of the hallmarks of journalism, and a challenging skill to learn, but it can also be a lot of fun. We recommend a logical approach:

- *Decide whom you will need to interview.* If you have been asked to pen an article about a resident in your community who has done something unusual or extraordinary, you will certainly need to interview that person. You may also want to talk to one or two of the person's family members or business associates, depending on the topic of your story. If the article is about a club or organization, you should speak to at least one leader of the organization, and perhaps one or two members to get a variety of viewpoints. Always interview more than one person when writing news articles; a good article includes information and quotes from multiple sources. Most importantly, especially for any controversial topics, be sure to get both sides of the story. Balanced reporting is key.

❖ *Brainstorm a list of questions to ask.* It helps to do some background research on the subject first. For example, if you are writing about an organization, check the Web site for information about its purpose, goals, membership, and so forth. Then come up with questions to ask in order to clarify and expand on what you've already learned. Include a mix of closed (yes/no) questions and open-ended questions that will invite your interviewee to elaborate.

❖ *Determine how best to conduct the interview.* In some cases, a phone or e-mail interview may be sufficient, if you don't have too many questions to ask. For longer interviews, or for discussions with a group of people, an in-person interview will be more beneficial.

Keep in mind that many publications do not allow their writers to conduct e-mail interviews, except for as a last resort or if a prominent individual requests an e-mail interview only. Some newspapers require reporters to clear the use of e-mail interviews with a managing editor. Simply put, e-mail, although it seems safe enough, is not a reliable mode of communication. E-mail allows those few dishonest people out there to embellish, cover-up, and sometimes lie about their answers and even their identities. Now, this is not to say that your sources aren't going to be honest—they almost always will be. But, newspapers are wary of e-mail interviews simply because the opportunity exists for dishonest people to take advantage of the situation. Most editors will always encourage you to try to set up an in-person or phone interview, with e-mail being your last resort.

If you do conduct an e-mail interview, you should begin with a brief summary of who you are, what newspaper you are writing for, and the article topic. Then provide a short list of questions. E-mail allows the interviewee to formulate responses on his or her own time, and it also makes quoting very easy for you, because you can simply copy and paste text from the response e-mail into your article. However, Danielle found that getting a timely response was sometimes difficult, and that can be a problem when you are on a deadline. It may help to give your interviewee a specific date by which to respond.

In most cases, though, a phone interview will probably be a better option than e-mail. This way you can have a live discussion with the other person, which gives you a chance to ask additional questions based on his responses. Again, begin by introducing yourself, what newspaper you work for, and the topic of the story. Then ask the person if now is a good time to talk. If not, arrange a time to call him or her back later.

Although an in-person interview is more time consuming than the others, it is generally the most effective. If your article is primarily about one person, by all means, interview him or her face-to-face. You should call in advance and arrange a place and time. For your safety, and the comfort of your interviewee, don't invite anyone to your home for an interview. In general, you should meet in a public place, like a park or coffee shop. If you are interviewing someone about her business or organization, consider meeting at her office. That way, she is more likely to have available all the information that she might need in order to answer your questions. She might also feel more comfortable in a familiar environment. Bring with you your list of questions and multiple pens (in case one dies during the interview), as well as a tape recorder and a camera if you can. Taping interviews helps you capture quotes accurately, but you should always be sure to take good, thorough notes, because you never know when you'll run out of tape, your batteries might die, or you may incur another form of technological malfunction. Your tapes should always serve as a backup to your good notes. It also doesn't hurt to take a few photos to accompany your article or ask your subject to bring a few with her.

❖ *Adapt to your subject's needs.* For any live discussion, whether over the phone or in person, make every effort to put your subject at ease. Many people understandably get nervous when interviewed by the press, so be polite and do your best to accommodate your subject's preferences and schedule. Also be flexible with your questions. If a question appears to make the person uncomfortable, don't press the matter; just move on. Conversely, if your interviewee provides an interesting response that you would like to explore further, ask additional questions in that direction.

Your initial list of prepared questions can get you started, but take advantage of the opportunity to have an active dialogue. Finally, stay objective and keep an open mind. Don't assume you know what your subject is going to say; give him or her your full attention.

Once you've finished your background research and interviews, it's time to pull together all of that information and do some actual writing. It's best to do this soon after the interviews while your memory is fresh. If you used a tape recorder, play it back while writing the story to fill in gaps and verify information and quotes. Insightful comments and personal anecdotes make great quotes, but keep an eye on their number and lengths. Too many will clutter your article, and long, rambling quotes may cause the reader to lose interest. You should paraphrase most of what your interviewees tell you, and only quote a few phrases or sentences that provide the most concise nuggets of information. Then, fact-check your article. If one of your interviewees made a statement outside of his or her expertise, back it up by confirming it with a reliable source. Avoid generalizations such as, "Many people believe. . . ." The information in your article should be as specific and solid as possible.

One quick way to double-check that your article contains all the key information is to look for the five W's: *who*, *what*, *where*, *when*, and *why*. If your piece does not answer all of these questions, you might be missing something. For example, if you are reporting on a specific event, you will want to describe who was involved in causing, planning, or attending the event; what was the nature of the event; where and when it occurred;

why it occurred; and why it is or will be important to your audience. Also, if it is relevant to your article, let the readers know where to look for more information if they are interested. For example, if you are writing about an organization, include contact information such as phone number, e-mail address, and/or Web site.

When editing your article, pay particular attention to the *lead*—the first couple of sentences. It needs to grab the reader's attention. To see some examples of good leads, peruse a recent edition of the newspaper, and read the first paragraph of each article. You'll notice that the style of the lead varies depending on the type of news story. For "hard news" articles—those covering current events or the issues of the day—the lead should succinctly summarize the key information about the topic. The rest of the article provides the details. For "soft news" articles—those that are not time sensitive, such as profiles of local residents or organizations—the lead can be more literary, alluding to the topic in a way that will pique the reader's interest.

Add a few paragraph breaks if necessary to keep your paragraphs short; otherwise, they will appear very long once your story is converted into the standard newspaper column format. Skim over your story to make sure that the quotes are dispersed more or less evenly throughout. Does the writing flow well in narrative form, with each paragraph leading the reader into the next? Finally, review the article with a critical eye for length. Relatively speaking, the editor will have an easier time finding space for shorter articles, so make sure you aren't going off into tangents or providing excessive detail on any one aspect of the topic. (If the editor does not provide an estimate of the target word count for a particular article, you may want to ask before you start writing it.) Particularly for your first few articles, it may be helpful to have them proofread by your English teacher, a member of your school newspaper staff, or a more experienced reporter working for the same newspaper.

Submit the completed article according to your editor's instructions a day or two before the official deadline if at all possible. When the article is printed, be sure to skim through it again to see if the editor has changed anything. By taking note of where the editor trims your articles or alters the wording, you can learn ways to improve your writing and make it more concise.

Writing for a local newspaper may present a few challenges:

- ✧ *Story topics you dislike*. Beware of speed bumps and be prepared for the occasional assignment that may not appeal to you.

- ✧ *Dealing with the public*. Any time you have to work with people you don't really know, you have to be prepared for a few glitches. Your interviewees may not always get back to you in a timely fashion, prompting you to call repeatedly to remind them that you still need to set up an interview or get some more information from them. On the other hand, you may also run into a few overbearing or mistrusting individuals who want to control how you write your article. Make sure you know the newspaper's policies about allowing subjects to approve articles before publication. Most major newspapers will not allow others outside of the editorial staff to read the article before it goes to print. In some cases, however, your editor may be willing to allow the subject to read only his or her direct quotes before the story has gone to press, to allow for the correction of any mistakes. Always check with your editor if a source insists on seeing the article or a copy of his or her quotes before it goes to print, as the policy varies from paper to paper. It's also a good idea to keep your notes from every interview you do, and in the case of a pesky source like the one above, you may also want to hold onto your tape-recorded interview.

❖ *Publication delays.* Don't get too attached to those short lead times. Occasionally, you may find that one of your articles gets postponed due to space constraints in the newspaper, or other factors. You should also be prepared for the possibility that one or two of your articles may never make it into print. Receiving a story assignment from an editor is not a guarantee that your article will be published.

❖ *Payment disproportionate to effort.* The payment you receive for an article may not always coincide with the time and effort required. Payment will most likely be based on the length of the article and the subject matter. Unfortunately, shorter articles sometimes actually require more effort. For example, Danielle was paid only $20 for her article on the city council meeting—despite having spent 4 hours at the meeting and a couple more writing the article—because the story was short and really only covered one issue (the speed bumps).

BECOMING AN EDITOR

Yes, this too is something you can do as a teenager or young adult; a great variety of editing opportunities exist, both online and in print. What's in it for you? The better question is, what's *not*? You will get insight into many different aspects of publishing: choosing photographs, designing layouts, editing the writing of others. Even if writing itself remains your favorite, experiencing these other behind-the-scenes activities will help you see the business from an editor's point of view—and that can only enhance your ability to give editors what they want in your freelancing. Additionally, in an editorial role, you have the power to influence what gets published. You learn to appreciate a variety of writing media and styles.

Aside from her yearbook staff efforts, Jessica had little experience with editing until she moved to Indianapolis after college. There, she joined the Society of Women Engineers' Central Indiana (SWE-CI) chapter and volunteered to be the sole editor of the online newsletter.

> By the time I graduated from college with my engineering degree, the right side of my brain was feeling sorely neglected, so I took the position as newsletter editor in order to reconnect with my love of writing. The *Indy Innovator* is published quarterly in PDF format and posted on the organization's Web site. About a month before each issue is supposed to come out, I send an e-mail to our 15 officers and committee chairs requesting newsletter inputs: announcements for upcoming events, reviews of conferences and luncheons, updates about SWE-CI activities, etc. Sound dry? I was a bit worried about that myself, so I've made a point of including a few "fun" pieces in each issue, such as an article on how to communicate with coworkers of the opposite sex.

I occasionally write articles myself, but most of my time is spent on other things. Being the editor means nagging people to send in their submissions on time, arranging the layout of the newsletter, obtaining photos and graphics, and, of course, editing everyone's writing. In most cases, that simply means fixing a few grammatical errors or reducing length, but I remember one article in particular that needed quite a bit of work. The author had some great insights to share, but she kept jumping from one idea to another, from good news to bad news and back again. The weak organizational structure made the article hard to follow. Resisting the temptation to overedit, I left most of her sentences intact—I just completely reshuffled their order. (This is one of many, many anecdotes that have made me wonder what people did before cut-and-paste was invented.)

So, what do I love about this job? Having influence over the big picture—content, style, visual appearance, finding the right balance among technical subjects, personal experiences of SWE-CI members, and a little humor. But, I am not without checks and balances, either. I always ask the officers to review issues before posting them, and when it comes to content, I do have people to answer to: the readers. The *Indy Innovator* is not *my* newsletter; it belongs to the 80 or 90 members of SWE-CI. As long as they're happy with my work, then I know I'm doing a good job with it.

~Jessica

So, if you are interested in being an editor, where should you look for opportunities? There are many different types of editing positions, and the skills and insights you gain will vary depending on which you choose. A few suggestions are included below.

Join Your School Literary Magazine Staff

If you prefer literary forms of writing, such as fiction or poetry, over journalism then your school's literary magazine staff may be the perfect forum in which to get your feet wet as an editor. In college, Danielle served on the staff of *University Blue*, Rice University's annual lit journal. Students, faculty, and alumni were all welcome to submit their stories, poems, personal essays, and visual art for consideration by the student editors. As submissions were received, the editors-in-chief would remove the authors' and artists' names for anonymity and distribute the pieces to the rest of the staff to review individually. Periodically, the staff would meet to discuss the merits of each submission and vote on which pieces to include in the magazine. The editors-in-chief would make the final selections from those pieces with the most "yes" votes, based on the amount of space available in the journal.

Deciding as a group what to publish can be a daunting task, largely because of the variations in perspective and personal taste from one staff member to the next. Danielle, for example, tended to prefer the funny, light-hearted pieces, while her fellow staff members often awarded more praise to the pensive work with darker tones. Nevertheless, a diverse editorial staff can greatly improve the quality of the finished product by providing a balanced variety of works to appeal to a broad student body audience. Compromises will be required, and you'll be outvoted at times, but if you feel very strongly about a submission one way or the other (and can explain the reasons for your opinion), don't be afraid to stand your ground.

Internal conflict can also make it difficult to decide on a piece. Danielle recalls one story in particular that presented a dilemma: It was an exceptionally vivid and graphic description of a girl's psychological disorder. Though the content was shocking and disturbing enough to make her hesitate about voting to publish it, the writing was excellent and evoked a strong emotional reaction. Editors have to make a lot of tough calls. In the end, that particular story made the cut and was published.

Keeping track of the production schedule is a challenge, too. There are a lot of steps involved in producing a literary magazine, from reading the submissions and making selections, to choosing fonts, arranging the pieces on the page, and designing the cover. If the staff spends too much time reviewing the submissions, the editors may have to rush through the layout process in order to meet the printers' deadline. Tackling these time constraints will give you valuable exposure to the hurdles that professional editors face.

Despite the challenges, being a literary magazine editor can be very rewarding. Even if you don't write any of the pieces yourself, you'll feel a sense of ownership for the total package, the finished magazine. You'll undoubtedly share some laughs with your fellow staffers. And, you may even gain some insights that will help you with your own writing.

Join Your School Yearbook or Newspaper Staff

A more journalistic option is to join your school yearbook or newspaper editorial staff. You don't necessarily have to be the editor-in-chief in charge of the whole production; more likely you would start out as a staff writer or reporter, then move on to be a section editor (e.g., editing all the sports articles). This type of editing mostly involves critiquing the work of other staff members, rather than sifting through a deluge of freelance submissions. You may have some level of authority over what gets published, but the editor-in-chief and/or faculty advisor will ultimately call the shots.

Perhaps the toughest thing about journalism is learning to be impartial. For example, in the interest of providing balanced coverage on both sides of some hot debate, you may have to publish opinions with which you utterly disagree. Or, you might have to rein in a writer whose personal bias on her latest topic is leaking into her just-the-facts article. If you're looking for a way to diversify the publication's perspective, try inviting other students who are not on the staff to submit articles or guest columns.

Impartiality also means being conscious of the variety of student interests and opinions. Avoid giving too much attention to what the popular kids are thinking and doing at the expense of other groups. This is especially complicated for the yearbook, because there's only one per year, and it's so permanent. When Jessica worked on her yearbook staff in college, one of her greatest difficulties lay in choosing photos. Because the most popular, outgoing students appeared in 80% of the pictures, she had to make a conscious effort to avoid devoting her whole section of the yearbook to these 15 or 20 highly visible people. As with yearbooks, it's also crucial to maintain balance in the school newspaper—if not within each issue, then at least over the course of the year. For example, if the school football team wins a championship, you might have most of one issue devoted to reports and interviews about the victory. That's fine, but then steer clear of sports in the next issue and focus on academics or other activities instead.

Also keep in mind that the field of journalism favors brevity and accuracy above flowery language. As an editor, you will spend much of your time fact-checking and trying to shrink word counts to get everything to fit on the page. You will learn to tailor articles into a straightforward, literal style with short sentences and short paragraphs—ideal for quick reading. The real challenge is to achieve these criteria without erasing creativity. A metaphor here and a colorful observation there can prevent an article from becoming too dry, while also maintaining readability.

If you yearn to be a reporter or want to stay on top of student opinion and school events, this is the place to be. Welcome to the world of late nights, pressing deadlines, and bad coffee. Now go start the presses!

Become the Sole Editor of a Specialized Local Publication

This is what Jessica has done with the Society of Women Engineers newsletter. Similarly, you might volunteer to take over as newsletter editor for a local religious group, start your own literary magazine, or publish and distribute community news updates. This type of editing is best for those who like to work independently and enjoy participating in all aspects of a project. Small publications like this are often a one-person job, which means you'll get to choose what to publish and when, create all the layouts, and do all the proofreading and fact-checking yourself. No small task, as you can imagine. But, then again, you'll also be the one everybody thanks when your first issue is the best one ever.

If your dream is to join the editorial staff of a larger publication, then working solo on a small newsletter is a very effective way to gain marketable experience. If you're the only person working on something, then your contribution to it will be broad and clearly visible, making it a great addition to your portfolio of published work.

Just make sure you have a reliable computer and are comfortable with the software you are using. There is nothing worse than that sinking feeling at 1 a.m. when your program freezes up for the eighth time just as you are putting the finishing touches on page 5. Trust us, we know.

Become the Web Master for a Club or Other Organization

There's a lot more to being a Web master than just editing—for starters, you will need to know (or be willing to learn) how to create and modify Web pages. But, if this appeals to you, then maintaining a Web site will also provide ample opportunity to write and edit announcements, articulate the goals of the organization, and post success stories. You may find that most of the other members of the club do not like writing (unless it's a writers' club, of course), so they won't necessarily send you stuff of their own volition. Instead, it will be up to you to decide what content is required and then ask (or possibly hound) the appropriate person to provide it. While this can be frustrating at times, it also means you get to create your own coherent vision for the Web site, rather than just posting a hodge-podge of whatever items people happen to send your way.

Another potential challenge of being a Web master—or blessing, depending on your personality—is the lack of concrete deadlines for making updates. When you take charge of a print publication, its very nature holds you accountable for providing current information to readers on a regular schedule, be it daily, weekly, or monthly. A Web page, on the other hand, is essentially continuous. You could update it multiple times a week, or let a month go by, depending on how much new information you have to share. If you are disciplined enough to update the Web site as needed, enjoy the flexibility. If not, serving as a Web master may not be the best fit for you. Leaving a Web page to languish with information that's months out of date will only send the message that your club or organization is lazy and disorganized, or worse, out of business.

Join the Editorial Board of a National Publication

Many publishers of teen and young adult magazines have acknowledged that the age difference between themselves and their readers can hinder them a bit in understanding and providing what their readers want. The solution? Collaborate with young editors. Let kids and teens have a say in what gets published.

This system has worked extraordinarily well for *New Moon*, a magazine for girls ages 8 to 14. Its Girls Editorial Board (GEB), consisting of about 15 girls, is involved in virtually all aspects of the publication. Check out the sidebar for insights from Lacey Louwagie, the assistant managing editor, and a few members of the GEB themselves.

Unfortunately, joining an editorial board like this usually necessitates living in the area where the magazine's offices are located. To apply for a spot on *New Moon*'s GEB, for instance, you would have to live in or near Duluth, MN. Luckily, a few magazines, such as *Speak Up*, maintain online editorial boards instead. In the case of *Speak Up*, teen editors login to an area of the Web site where submissions are posted for their review. (Unfortunately, *Speak Up* is currently not accepting submissions, but keep your eyes open for its return.) Regardless of whether they are conducted in person or online, be prepared to face a great deal of competition to become involved in national magazines' editorial boards. But, don't hesitate to apply either, if this is something you really want.

How can you find publications that collaborate with young editors? Start by checking the mastheads in the magazines you like to see if they give credit to an editorial board. Flip through the pages to see if there are any announcements about starting a board. You can also try looking at magazines' Web sites. Typically the Web site or a notice in the magazine will also explain the application process, at least if the publication is currently taking applications. Or, you might try e-mailing the editors to express your interest. How to increase your chances of being offered a position? The best way may be to write for the magazine as a freelancer first. This will hopefully give you some name recognition among the staff and will also demonstrate that you have a strong grasp on the magazine's style and content.

NEW MOON'S **GIRLS EDITORIAL BOARD**

In May 2005, Lacy Louwagie, the assistant managing editor at *New Moon*, offered us an in-depth look at the GEB.

Q. What is the role of the board in producing the magazine?

A. The Girls Editorial Board makes all the major decisions about the content of the magazine—choosing which articles, letters, stories, and artwork to print; interviewing subjects; choosing cover art; and editing articles and cartoons. At the Girls Editorial Board [biweekly] meetings, . . . the adult editors and the girl editors work as peers—we both have strengths that we bring to the table and our strengths are valued equally. We discuss issues and we vote. . . .Then the adult staff works throughout the week to make sure the decisions made at the meeting are implemented into the final product. Girls Editorial Board members also serve as representatives of *New Moon* and are often asked to speak at or attend conferences. Furthermore, they give feedback about big company decisions such as marketing—but their main priority and sphere of influence is the magazine.

Q. How do you choose board members? Do current members get involved in picking new ones?

A. The current members are incredibly involved in the entire process. . . . We have conversations about the strengths the current board has and what strengths may be lacking. Because the GEB makes decisions that affect many, many readers, it's important that the GEB represent a very diverse sampling of girls. . . . We look for diversity of age, race, religion, and life experiences, so [our needs] at any given time might shift. One thing that remains constant is that we want girls who are dedicated to *New Moon* and like to read, write, and discuss. We bring new girls onto the board every spring. . . . Out of all the applications we get, we choose to interview a few girls, [then accept] between two and six girls per spring. The current GEB members conduct the interviews and make the final decisions.

Q. What percentage of applicants is accepted to join the board?

A. We usually get about 50 applications and have about 3 spots open—so that figures down to an average of 6%. Again, that number can fluctuate depending on the amount of openings.

Q. What advice would you give to girls interested in joining?

A. Read *New Moon*. Become familiar with our magazine and with our mission. When you fill out an application, be unique— don't be afraid to tell us exactly who you are.

We also asked a few questions of the girls themselves, and received the following responses from GEB members Kelly, 14, Carley, 14, and Charina, 13.

Q. What made you want to do this?

A. Heard about it through school. . . . Read *New Moon* at the library, thought it was a cool magazine with good messages. . . . We hear a lot of girls complaining about the media—like that we have to look pretty, but most girls don't do anything about it, that's why I wanted to be on the board—so I could actually *do* something, instead of just sitting on the couch.

Q. What is your work method? How do you communicate with other editors?

A. We brainstorm and discuss everything and are on a first-name basis with the adult editors. We work on big decisions in large groups (like cover art and brainstorming ideas) and work in small groups to choose letters to print and edit articles.

Q. What advice would you offer to other girls interested in joining?

A. You need to live near enough to Duluth, MN, to come to the meetings twice a month. Think about what you want to get out of the experience, what kind of change you want to influence. Research *New Moon* so you know what kind of commitment you're in for. Have fun, and be yourself!

Work in a Publication's Editorial Department as an Intern

This is a bit different from joining an editorial board in the sense that you may be the only teen (or one of only two or three) involved in the production. Additionally, while editorial boards exist chiefly to offer insight from a reader's point of view, the main purpose of an internship is usually for the intern to gain work experience while completing necessary tasks for the publication. An intern's role may include copy-editing, responding to mail and e-mail, assisting with layouts, and so forth. Your level of authority in decision making will also vary. For instance, you may serve as the initial screener of all submissions received and can share your opinion about which ones you'd accept, but ultimately you may or may not have significant influence over what gets printed. Either way, though, an editorial internship will offer a unique inside look at how periodicals are published. You'll get to sit in on staff meetings and see how decisions are made.

Skipping Stones, a cultural magazine based in Oregon, hires an average of five student interns per year to work in the editorial offices and read submissions. In addition, *Skipping Stones* has several student reviewers who critique whole issues; they evaluate the content, layout, flow of material, and so forth. Interested students should send a letter to the editors and enclose a few samples of their writing. *BUILD* magazine, based in New York City, also offers unpaid journalism/editorial internships.

As with editorial boards, check magazines' mastheads and Web sites to see if they offer internships. Of course, becoming an intern requires that you live near the editorial offices. Fortunately, not all magazines are based in New York City (even though it sure seems like it sometimes). If you live in or near a major metropolitan area, you may find at least a couple of open positions. Try searching an online directory (e.g., http://www.yellowpagesnationwide.com) to find out if there are any publishing offices nearby. As we mentioned above in reference to teen editorial boards, writing for a magazine as a freelancer first may improve your chances of landing an internship. In this case, prior work experience will also help, especially any office positions you may have held.

Challenges of Being an Editor

Regardless of the type of editorial position you are looking for, some of the challenges are universal. You may relish learning the ins and outs of the publishing business, but you will also get to find out why editors are so often frazzled. Welcome to the world of deadlines and tough decisions. Be prepared for the following:

❖ *Struggling to remain objective or impartial.* Your own personal tastes may not always align with what appeals to your readers, so you may not like every piece you publish. You will need the ability to recognize and appreciate the merit in submissions that suit the needs of your audience but may seem uninteresting or aggravating to you personally.

❖ *Maintaining balance in the content.* The interests and opinions of your readers may vary widely, and this should be reflected in the publication. Depending on the nature of the audience, you may need to address the wishes of both men and women, readers of different ages or ethnic backgrounds, people who want entertainment and those who want news, and so forth. It helps if you work with other editors whose interests and viewpoints differ from yours, because this will provide more balanced judgment about what to print. (Your teamwork and negotiation skills will get some serious exercise, too.)

❖ *Resisting the temptation to overedit.* Especially in creative publications, editors need to show restraint when revising submissions, so as not to erase the unique style of the writer. There's a difference between editing for grammar, clarity, and length versus rewording something just because it doesn't conform to the way you would have written it. You may think the whole thing would sound better if it were written in your style, but refrain—for the writer's sake, and the readers'.

❖ *Dealing with space limitations.* Ever had to explain something in 500 words or fewer, but ended up with 512 and just could *not* find anything to cut? Get ready to face that a lot as an editor, especially if you don't have the leeway to alter font sizes or margins. And, that's after you've already eliminated several praiseworthy pieces just to keep from being several *pages* over your limit. On the plus side, you will see for yourself that many highly deserving submissions don't get accepted due to space limitations; this may help you put your own freelance-writing rejection pile into perspective.

WHAT ABOUT BOOK PUBLISHING?

Perhaps some of you are frustrated by now, wondering why we have been focusing almost exclusively on writing for periodicals. "But, I want to write *books*!" you might be thinking. "How do I publish books?"

Let's start by stating an unfortunate, but kind of understandable, fact: Very few book publishers are interested in work by young writers. By and large, it is much easier for a teenager, or a writer of any age, to contribute to a magazine than to publish an entire book. On the other hand, we would be the *last* people on earth to tell you that it can't be done. It most certainly can, and we encourage you to pursue it relentlessly if that is your dream. Just be prepared for a serious challenge.

Why don't more books by young people get published? For one thing, book publishing carries greater risks—the publisher invests a lot of money up front in preparing and printing the book, and if it doesn't sell well, the company could ultimately lose money on it. This is why first-time book authors, regardless of their age, have a notoriously difficult time getting attention from the likes of Random House and Simon & Schuster. Many of the largest companies won't even read submissions sent directly by the authors; they work only with agents, which very few young writers have. (The adage is that you can't get a book published unless you have an agent to vouch for you, but you can't get an agent until you've published at least one book—a classic catch-22.) Publishers also tend to assume (here's the unfair part) that teens are immature and inexperienced writers, so it would never occur to them to encourage teen submissions. Book publishing may also carry additional responsibility for the author, such as participating in book signings, media appearances, and other promotional activities. Being in school, teenagers would likely have more difficulty finding the time for such things than an adult who writes for a living.

Even now, as we are working on the second edition, we both have trouble believing how lucky we were to ever get this book into print. But, our approach was pretty clever: After a couple of years of writing occasional pieces for *Creative Kids* magazine, we found out that the company, Prufrock Press, also prints books. Right away, it seemed like the most promising market. The staff was accustomed to communicating with young writers and fully recognized their talents. The magazine and our book had the same target audience. And, given the number of submissions we had each sent to *Creative Kids* during the past couple of years, there was a good chance our names would look familiar when they received the book query. The powers that be didn't let us down, and the rest is history.

So, how can you improve your chances of getting a book published? Here are some thoughts:

❖ *Be prepared to compete with adults*. For example, if you'd like to write a young adult novel, you will probably want to submit it to large publishers that usually get adult submissions. Keep in mind that you are not obligated to disclose your age when you submit the proposal. If you don't, your work will then be judged entirely on its merit compared to other submissions by novelists of all ages.

❖ *Use your age to your advantage*. If you are writing a nonfiction book specifically targeted to teens, or to people who are trying to understand teens, then you will definitely want to advertise that you *are* a teen. That fact will help your book stand out from others on the same topic. The book you are now holding is a case in point. Another excellent example is *Breaking the Code: Two Teens Reveal the Secrets to Better Parent-Child Communication* (2005) written by Lara Fox and Hilary Frankel, two high school students in New York (see sidebar). The book gives advice to

BREAKING INTO PRINT: AN INTERVIEW WITH TEEN BOOK AUTHORS

Though most nonfiction books follow roughly the same process of publication, the experience is a little bit different for every author. Our case may not have been that typical, because we did not write an official book proposal, work with an agent, nor pitch our book to multiple publishing houses. To give you another perspective, we interviewed Hilary Frankel and Lara Fox, authors of *Breaking the Code*, a book for parents on how to communicate effectively with their teenage offspring. Hilary and Lara were in high school when they wrote the book and had it published by New American Library (NAL), a division of Penguin.

Q: What gave you the idea to write *Breaking the Code*?

A: A psychologist was invited to speak to parents at our high school about parent-child communication and the teenager's thought process. We found this interesting because although a psychologist can take an educated guess on what a teenager is thinking, it is still a guess. [As teens ourselves], we realized that we wouldn't have to interpret the teenager's thought process; we could translate it for the parents.

Q: Did either of you have any writing or publishing experience before you wrote *Breaking the Code*? If so, did it help you as you were writing and marketing the book?

A: Both of us had written extensively in high school, but only English and history essays and that sort of thing. Neither of us had ever published anything before, but for our book all we needed to do was stay true to the teenage voice and experience; the writing flowed easily because it was simple transcribing the things we and our friends were living every day.

Q: Do you have an agent? If so, how did you find and work with him or her?

A: One day in art class, we were talking about our book idea with a bunch of friends when our teacher, Nancy Fried, overheard us. She asked us what we were talking about, and we described the project. As it turns out, her sister, Alice Martell, is a well-known literary agent in New York, and a parent of two teenagers. Nancy mentioned the book idea to her sister, and [she] was very intrigued by it. We contacted her and set up a meeting. From the beginning, she was enthusiastic about our idea and gave us the confidence to move forward with the project. She explained the basics of approaching publishing houses and told us that we needed to write a proposal and sample chapter. Without her guidance we wouldn't have pulled off this project.

Q: How did you go about finding potential publishers? What led you to NAL?

A: We wrote a complete proposal for the book, which talked about the unique perspective we would bring to the issue of parenting and outlined all the chapters and issues we planned to cover in the book. We also wrote a sample chapter so publishers could see our style and understand the importance of the teenage voice. After [we wrote] the proposal and sample chapter, our agent sent out copies to all the major publishing houses. We set up meetings with three of the interested publishers in New York. NAL was actually the first meeting we had, and we ended up on the same page as the editors there. They understood what our book was about and believed in it, and so we agreed to work with them.

Q: Once the manuscript was accepted, what was the revision process like? How much control did you have over any changes?

A: The entire time that we were writing the manuscript we were in contact with our editor at NAL. She would read chunks of the book and send back line edits and other suggestions as we went along. There were never any major rewrites because we had an open dialogue with the editor about how the book should read and be structured and everyone understood that the teenager's voice needed to stay strong throughout the book. Of course, the final manuscript was then line edited again.

Q: Collaborating as coauthors can be difficult at times (we know from experience!). How did you two balance the workload or divide up responsibilities?

A: We wrote the entire book together at Lara's desk. For 6 months during our junior year in high school, we dedicated every Saturday to writing. Our deadline was a week after the SAT test and right before final exams. Once we had our outline drawn up, we set deadlines for ourselves, so each week we had a new section to complete. That's what kept us focused.

parents on how to communicate with their teens—a topic that Fox and Frankel have inside knowledge about, being teens themselves. Similarly, 15-year-old Nora Coon published *Teen Dream Jobs: How to Find the Job You Really Want* in 2003.

❖ *Get some experience first by writing for magazines.* This will help you on so many levels. You will gain an understanding of the publishing industry and freelancing in general, you can hone your writing talents by working on shorter pieces, and you can advertise yourself as a published writer when you submit your book proposal. The more success and experience you can point to, the better you will look in the eyes of the publisher.

❖ *Look for publishers that have had some experience working with young writers.* They are more likely to look past your age and recognize your talents. Find out if your favorite magazine publishers carry books, as well. If you find other books by teens in the bookstore, check to see who published them. Search the Internet—you might find a lead.

❖ *If you have the time, money, determination, and entrepreneurial spirit, try self-publishing the book first.* You may have heard of Christopher Paolini, author of the novel *Eragon*.

According to an interview printed in *The Christian Science Monitor*, the 19-year-old Paolini self-published the book with the help of his parents. Having obtained his high school diploma (via GED) at the age of 15, Paolini delayed going to college and instead devoted his time to traveling the country promoting the book. After he sold 10,000 copies of it this way, it was picked up by Alfred A. Knopf publishing house in 2003. (Self-publishing will be discussed further a little later in the chapter.)

A list of book publishing opportunities can be found in Appendix B.

Market Search

Regardless of whether you want to approach some of the publishers we suggest (see Appendix B) or look elsewhere, you will need to do some serious market research to find the most promising targets. As with magazines, book publishers usually limit their products to one target audience or certain subject areas. For example, Free Spirit focuses on self-help books for kids and teenagers, while Prufrock Press specializes in gifted education. Therefore, before you submit a proposal to any publisher, it is crucial that you study its catalog to understand what kinds of books it publishes. You might also benefit from perusing some of its books at the library or bookstore to learn about the publisher's preferred writing style or philosophical approach to the subject. You don't want your book to be *too* similar to the publisher's other titles (if it doesn't fill a gap, why should it be published?), but you do need to be able to convince the editor that your manuscript would be an excellent fit for the company's catalog.

You should also research your competition. Look for other books that resemble yours, regardless of who published them. What sets yours apart? Is it more imaginative? Better organized? Will it appeal to a specific niche audience whose needs or interests similar books have ignored? Depending on your topic, this is also where being a teenager could work to your advantage, as we discussed above. If you find that the market is already flooded with books that cover the same territory as yours, then your best hope is to change direction a bit and find a way to make it more unique. Either that, or start over with a different topic altogether.

You might want to hold off on writing the entire manuscript at least until you've done your research. This advice applies especially well to nonfiction books, but may be smart for fiction, as well. Your vision for the book you want to write may morph a great deal through the market research process. In fact, it is often best to wait until you find a publisher who likes your proposal and expresses interest in seeing the complete manuscript. Otherwise, you might end up devoting an enormous amount of time and energy to a book that never gets published. We found this out for ourselves through an attempt to publish a compilation of fun facts, myths, and puzzles about the solar system. We wrote almost 100 pages only to find that no one was interested, mostly because the book's hodge-podge concept was flawed in the first place. So, keep that in mind while you are searching for a market for your ideas.

Book Publishing Submission Process

The typical submission process for books also differs from that of magazines. The key difference is that book publishers often do not look at an entire manuscript up front. Instead, authors and/or their agents submit book proposals, which provide an outline of the book's contents, as well as samples of their writing.

Once you've identified a publisher to pursue, read the submission guidelines. Unless they specify that you must submit a complete book proposal with your initial correspondence, we'd recommend that you start with a simple query letter explaining the basic concept of the book. This way you can wait until a publisher shows interest before you put the effort into creating a detailed proposal. You must keep your query letter short (no more than a page) if you expect a busy editor to actually read it. Regardless of whether you are writing fiction or nonfiction, start by briefly describing your book's target audience and discussing how it would fit in with the publisher's other titles. Also include the following:

- *Nonfiction queries.* Here's your chance to floor the editor with all that research you've been doing. Explain the book's purpose. How will it compare to similar ones already on the market? Name specific competitors, and elaborate on how your book will stand apart from them. What makes your approach unique? Who is your target audience, and why will they buy *your* book? Also describe your credentials as an author. What makes you an "expert" on your book's subject? Do you have any previous publishing experience, especially on similar topics? For example, if you've been writing a column about school sports for a youth publication for the past year, and are now proposing a book on the same subject, be sure to mention the column in your query letter.

❖ *Fiction queries.* Discuss the plot, themes, and characters. Why would your target audience want to read this story? The goal here is to intrigue the editor so that she will want to read the manuscript. But, don't be too coy either—go ahead and divulge the ending. (Why, you ask? Think of it this way: How many novels have you read that seemed promising in Chapter 1, but concluded with a predictable or preposterous ending? An editor wants some assurance that she will not encounter this when she reads your manuscript.)

If your query letter leaves an impression on the editor, he or she may request a more in-depth book proposal from you. Or, you may have skipped the query letter step if the publisher's guidelines indicated a preference for receiving a whole proposal up front. Either way, book proposals usually include the following (requirements vary, so check the publisher's guidelines):

❖ *A cover letter.* If this is your first contact with the editor, the cover letter should include the same content as described above for query letters. If the editor has already seen a query letter from you and has requested further information, then the cover letter should simply thank him or her for showing interest and briefly list the materials enclosed.

❖ *A detailed outline.* For nonfiction, include working titles for each of the chapters and a brief description of the contents.

For fiction, summarize the plot. The outline (typically two–three pages long) should leave the editor with a very clear idea of the contents or plot structure of the book.

❖ *Sample pages or sample chapter.* Include the text of at least one fully developed chapter to demonstrate your writing style. Again, editors are very busy people, so don't overdo it—5 to 10 pages are enough.

As you can see, putting together a book proposal requires a fairly significant investment of time and effort. Once you have assembled it, you may find it helpful to submit it to a critique service, such as that offered by the SouthWest Writers, for feedback on your book concept, writing style, and the overall presentation of your proposal. To test out the SouthWest Writers' service, we managed to dig up and send in an old proposal we had written for another book project. The editor offered useful advice on how to structure a proposal (some of which has been incorporated into our suggestions above), suggested a resource specific to book proposals, and provided several comments on the content and tone of the sample chapter we submitted.

Check your local library or bookstore for resources that discuss book publishing in detail. The annual *Children's Writer's and Illustrator's Market*, for example, is a popular guidebook for writers of children's books and teen/young adult books. This and other resources can help you find an agent, research markets, and write book proposals. For an online resource, try the Society of Children's Book Writers and Illustrators (see http://www.scbwi.org), which offers writing exercises, discussion boards, and a bimonthly bulletin for members. Also look for opportunities to get firsthand advice from as many published book authors as you can find. Attend book signings and readings at your local library or bookstore, or join online forums and chat rooms for writers.

SELF-PUBLISHING

The most straightforward way to see your work in print—and admittedly, one of the most difficult—is to submit it to a professional magazine, newspaper, or commercial book publisher in hopes that they will accept it for publication. Thus far we have focused on this traditional approach because it is the foundation of freelance publishing and remains highly rewarding. However, the landscape has changed dramatically over the last several years, and the alternative of self-publishing has expanded and grown increasingly popular.

Self-publishing is just what it sounds like—the act of publishing something yourself. This could be as simple as using desktop publishing software on your computer to format and print out copies of your work and distributing them to neighbors and friends. The most common example, particularly among adult writers, is to create a novel or nonfiction book and pay a print shop to produce copies of it for you to distribute. Regardless, in self-publishing, you do most of the work and are responsible for the entire process: writing, editing, designing layouts and graphics or illustrations, marketing, and distributing copies of the finished product. You retain all rights to the work, and all proceeds belong to you.

Obviously, this kind of self-publishing is not for everyone. It's really a business in and of itself, requiring a true entrepreneurial spirit and a significant investment of time and money, particularly if you are self-publishing a book. It's hard to make a profit when you have to pay for something to be printed in the first place. Without the assistance of professional editors and graphic artists, your work may not reach its full potential. Also, some people equate self-publishing with self-indulgence. They may assume—rightfully or not—that you chose to publish your work yourself because it wasn't "good enough" to be accepted by a "real" publisher, or because you didn't have the patience to collaborate with an editorial staff. Impatience certainly is not a good reason to self-publish.

However, thanks to the advent of digital or electronic means of publishing, self-publishing has become much more popular, and much more affordable than it used to be. One such approach is print-on-demand (POD), in which the printer produces copies of the book as orders are placed, rather than printing a set number of copies up front and then trying to sell them. This greatly reduces the risk of a failed investment if the book does not perform well on the market. Print-on-demand and E-publishing firms such as iUniverse, AuthorHouse, and Xlibris may charge the author approximately $500 to $1,000 to publish a book.

A handful of talented (and lucky) authors have managed to generate bestsellers by self-publishing, including Amanda Brown and Richard N. Bolles with *Legally Blonde* (2001) and *What Color is Your Parachute?* (1970), respectively. If a self-published book sells enough copies, thereby proving that it has a substantial audience, it may get the attention of traditional book publishers. The author may then land a contract with one of these big publishers to reprint the book. Although this type of success story is still rare, it has helped change the reputation of self-publishing, making it more respectable in the industry.

There's even an annual contest called the DIY Book Festival (for "Do It Yourself"), currently in its fifth year, that exists to honor exceptional self-published books in several categories, including fiction, nonfiction, children's books, and e-books. The grand prize is $1,000 in cash. There is a $50 entrance fee, but this includes admission to the DIY Convention, which offers workshops and information on how to create, promote, and distribute self-published books (for more information, see http://www.diyconvention.com).

Self-publishing can offer a great opportunity for an author whose work doesn't quite fit with a mainstream publisher. Examples include a detailed family history, a book of family recipes, or a collection of your previously published works (just make sure you still retain the rights to each piece). These subjects may appeal to your relatives and friends, but not to a mass audience. Self-publishing may also provide an outlet for ideas that fall "outside the box." First, however, take a step back and try to give yourself, and your ego, an honest appraisal. Are you looking to self-publish simply because you are afraid of receiving criticism from an editor or can't stand to make compromises with a traditional publisher? Or, are you genuinely interested in taking charge of the whole process in order to bring your unique project to life? Do you have the time and energy to commit to the project? Can you afford it? It helps to have the support of your family and friends, as well.

If self-publishing is a path you really want to pursue, you will need to research the details of the process. Check your local library or bookstore for resources that focus on this subject. A few are also listed in the back of this book (see Additional Resources).

CHAPTER 5:
(NOT YOUR ORDINARY)
DIRECTORY OF MARKETS

• • • • • • • • • • • • • • • • • • • •

PUBLICATIONS: PRINT AND ONLINE

At last, the long-awaited market list. Rest assured that the list below is not just a hodgepodge of random youth publications. We did our homework and selected only the best opportunities in print and online. Included with each listing is contact information, a list of what the magazine publishes, key details of the submission process, and suggestions and insights from the editors, as well as from us. As always, it will be necessary to request writer's guidelines or look them up online before submitting your work to any publication. These listings are intended simply to help you select markets to pursue further.

If you take a moment to flip through the directory, you might feel that it's a bit short. This is actually by design. In assembling our list, we started out with more than 80 markets, and then eliminated those that had gone out of business and whittled the rest down to 20. We did this by ordering sample copies of print publications, pouring over Web sites, and sending detailed questionnaires to the editors. As a result, you won't find photocopied newsletters or unattractive "database" Web sites on this list. We've made a point of presenting you with the most promising and rewarding outlets for young writers.

A quick note about content: Please be aware that some of the magazines and Web sites listed in this directory have been known to publish profanity, though not pervasively. Therefore, some content found in some of these publications may not be appropriate for younger aspiring writers.

Finally, we leave you with three essential reminders. As obvious as they may seem, clearly some young writers are not following them, because we hear these from editors all of the time:

- ❖ Do not ever submit your first draft. Only send your best, polished work.
- ❖ Read back issues. You'll be much more successful once you find a magazine that really suits your style.
- ❖ *Always* follow the guidelines.

PUBLICATION ADDRESS	***The Apprentice Writer*** c/o Gary Fincke, Writers Institute Director Box GG Susquehanna University Selinsgrove, PA 17870 gfincke@susqu.edu
WEB ADDRESS	http://www.susqu.edu/writers/High SchoolStudents.htm
IN A NUTSHELL	*The Apprentice Writer* is an annual literary publication by and for high school students. The publication is black and white and 60 pages in length. Edited and produced in part by Susquehanna University writing students, it is distributed in September each year.
INDUSTRY PRESENCE	Established in 1982. Circulation: 11,000.
WORKS PUBLISHED	Poetry, fiction, personal essays, and photography by students in grades 9–12.
THE ODDS	100% written by teens. Approximately 2% of all submissions are published.
TIMELINE	Submissions are due at the beginning of March each year. The publication responds by early May to accepted authors only. The magazine is distributed in September.
RIGHTS AND COMPENSATION	Magazine takes first rights. Published authors and their teachers receive a complimentary copy of the publication.

SAMPLE COPY	E-mail Dr. Gary Fincke at gfincke@susqu. edu.
SUBMISSION PROCESS	Mail submissions to Dr. Gary Fincke at the mailing address above.
ADVICE FROM THE EDITORS	Common mistakes include explaining too much, providing all plot and no characters, and using too many clichés. Remember to include your name and address on the manuscript. The editors receive too many rhymed sentimental poems and genre stories such as fantasy and science fiction. Read a few back issues to get a sense of what they are looking for.
OUR IMPRESSIONS	This anthology has the look and feel of a newspaper, only with poetry and prose in place of news and ads. Most of the pieces are thoughtful and reflective in tone; the glimmers of humor lean toward wry musings rather than the laugh-out-loud variety.
WORKSHOP OPPORTUNITY	Susquehanna University, located in Pennsylvania, offers an annual week-long Writers Workshop in the summer. Experienced writers are eligible to attend the summer before they begin 11th or 12th grade (see Chapter 3 for more information on workshops).

PUBLICATION	***BUILD: The Magazine By and For Young People Changing Their World***
ADDRESS	Do Something 24-32 Union Square East, 4th Floor South New York, NY 10003 editor@dosomething.org
WEB ADDRESS	http://www.dosomething.org
IN A NUTSHELL	*BUILD* is a full color national magazine devoted to youth activism in the areas of community building, health, and the environment. There are three issues per year and the issues are 26 pages in length. Also publishes articles online, and the online content is updated every 1–2 weeks.
INDUSTRY PRESENCE	Established in 1995; ceased publication in 1998; relaunched in 2005. Print circulation: 220,000.
WORKS PUBLISHED	Informative/motivating articles, interviews with teens making a difference, personal essays—all having to do with community, health, or the environment.
THE ODDS	Approximately 85% of the magazine is written by youth, ages 13–23. Publishes about 80% of submissions received. All accepted articles are published either in print or online, not both.

TIMELINE	Responds to accepted work only, typically within a few days. Lead time is 6–8 weeks for print and 1–3 weeks online.
RIGHTS AND COMPENSATION	All submissions (accepted or not) typically become the exclusive property of the publisher, although the author may request an exception if his or her work is rejected. There is no payment, but copies are available for free.
SAMPLE COPY	Free. E-mail request (include desired number of copies and your mailing address) to the address above. The magazine is also available at Sam Goody stores.
SUBMISSION PROCESS	E-mail the *BUILD* editor at the e-mail address above.
ADVICE FROM THE EDITORS	Managing Editor Emily Luke writes, "Ask someone to proofread your work before you submit it. Also, make sure your story is engaging—you want other youth to be interested in what you have to say. This isn't English class—you don't need to make your article sound like an essay, there is no maximum or minimum length (within reason), and we want you to have fun writing for us."
OUR IMPRESSIONS	*BUILD* has a refreshingly upbeat attitude, and we love that it's dedicated to showcasing teens' potential to impact society in positive ways. The conversational tone and

wide variety of discussed activities (big and small) suggest that any teen can support a cause and share his or her experiences with others. *BUILD* also offers unpaid editorial internships.

PUBLICATION	***Cicada***
ADDRESS	315 Fifth Street
	Peru, IL 61354
WEB ADDRESS	http://www.cricketmag.com
IN A NUTSHELL	This is a literary magazine for young adults (ages 14 and up). The 128-page publication is black and white with color cover and is perfect bound. There are six issues per year.
INDUSTRY PRESENCE	Established in 1998. Circulation: 18,000.
WORKS PUBLISHED	Fiction, nonfiction (personal experiences), opinion pieces/essays for the "Expressions" feature, poetry, book reviews, and black-and-white artwork.
THE ODDS	25–30% of the magazine is written by teens. Approximately 1–5% of all submissions are published.
TIMELINE	The response time is 12 weeks. Lead time is approximately 6–8 months.
RIGHTS AND COMPENSATION	The magazine takes all rights. Authors receive a cash payment upon publication.
SAMPLE COPY	*Cicada* is carried in many bookstores. You can find submission guidelines in the back of the magazine.
SUBMISSION PROCESS	Mail to Submissions Editor at the address above. Do not e-mail submissions.

ADVICE FROM THE EDITORS

Executive Editor Deborah Vetter notes, "Common mistakes for poetry include dense, overwritten verse; simplicity has its virtues! For stories, we sometimes find that teens write beyond their experience. We're seeing a lot of dark, serious writing and would like more humor and less angst." They also would like to receive more first-person essays for the "Expressions" feature.

OUR IMPRESSIONS

Cicada is refreshingly ad-free. Most of the magazine is text, but the stories are illustrated. Content-wise, *Cicada* makes an effort to represent a variety of cultures and backgrounds. Based on its professional design and the quality of the writing, we consider this to be one of the best literary magazines out there for teens.

FEEDBACK OPPORTUNITY

The Slam is a selective online forum to which teens and young adults (ages 14–23) can submit their microfiction (very short fiction) and poetry for critique by other teens. Some of the best Slam submissions may be chosen for publication in *Cicada*. To get to the Slam page, go to http://www.cricket-mag.com and follow the link. Submissions for The Slam must be sent via an online form.

PUBLICATION	***The Claremont Review***
ADDRESS	4980 Wesley Road
	Victoria, BC V8Y 1Y9
	Canada
WEB ADDRESS	http://www.theClaremontReview.ca
IN A NUTSHELL	This is a literary anthology by and for teens (ages 13–19) that is published twice a year (spring and fall). The 120-page magazine has a color cover with black-and-white interior and is perfect bound.
INDUSTRY PRESENCE	Established in 1991. Circulation: 1,000.
WORKS PUBLISHED	Short stories, poetry, black-and-white graphic art and photography, and short plays.
THE ODDS	100% of the magazine is written by teens. Approximately 10% of all submissions are published.
TIMELINE	Response time ranges from 4 weeks to 4 months depending on time of year (winter is faster).
RIGHTS AND COMPENSATION	Magazine takes first rights on unpublished work. Complimentary copy for published authors.
SAMPLE COPY	For the current issue, the price is $12 Canadian or the equivalent in U.S. funds (varies with exchange rate). For past issues,

SUBMISSION
PROCESS

ADVICE FROM
THE EDITORS

price is $7 U.S. or Canadian. Send check or money order to the address above.

Mail to the editors at the address above. Do not e-mail submissions.

The Claremont Review is looking for work that reveals something of the human condition. It is not looking for science fiction, fantasy, or romance. It accepts very little rhyming poetry. They would like to receive more art submissions but generally publish no more than 5 per issue, including cover art. All submissions accompanied by a SASE will receive a personal response with comments. Editor Susan Stenson writes, "Concentrate on clear, crisp sentences, developed characters, well-edited poems that are rich in sound and theme. We really are in need of good, solid fiction. Much of what we receive has no scenes, little dialogue, and no exposition." She also recommends being persistent. If your work is rejected, revise it and send it back, addressed to the same editor who responded originally. Finally, a reminder to American writers: Do not put U.S. postage stamps on your SASE. Use Canadian stamps or enclose an International Reply Coupon (IRC).

OUR IMPRESSIONS

The writing in *The Claremont Review* is high quality—the kind of pieces you want to read more than once to peel apart the layers of meaning. Brief (and often amusing) author biographies are included at the end. These, and a few humorous poems and stories, are especially satisfying as they help to balance the more serious majority of the pieces. We love that the editors take the time to send a personal response with comments to all writers who submit. The magazine's Web site also offers writing tips from the editors and published authors.

CONTEST OPPORTUNITY

The Claremont Review holds an annual writing contest for fiction and poetry. Winners are published in the fall issue, and cash prizes are awarded. The entry fee buys a one-year subscription to the publication.

FEEDBACK OPPORTUNITIES

The Claremont Review offers a professional critique service, as well as a Mentors in Writing program (see Chapter 3 for details).

PUBLICATION ADDRESS	***Creative Kids Magazine*** P.O. Box 8813 Waco, TX 76714-8813 CK@prufrock.com
WEB ADDRESS	http://www.prufrock.com
IN A NUTSHELL	This is a national magazine by and for kids ages 8–14 published four times each year. It has a two-color interior and a full-color cover.
INDUSTRY PRESENCE	Established in 1981. Circulation: 6,000.
WORKS PUBLISHED	Stories, poetry, photographs, artwork, activities, editorials, articles, essays, plays, puzzles/games—any type of creative work that can fit in the magazine.
THE ODDS	100% of the magazine is written by kids and teens. Approximately 5% of all submissions are published.
TIMELINE	Response time is approximately 6–8 weeks. Lead time up to 2 years.
RIGHTS AND COMPENSATION	Magazine holds reprint rights, and the author retains copyright. Complimentary copy for published authors.
SAMPLE COPY	Mail $3.75 to the address above.
SUBMISSION PROCESS	Mail to Submissions Editor at the address above. Do not e-mail submissions. Editor Jennifer Robins writes, "We are look-

**ADVICE FROM
THE EDITORS**

ing for work from students who are thinking 'outside of the box.' The more creative
the submission, the better. Submissions
that do not follow the guidelines are dis-
carded, so be sure to review the guidelines
before submitting work." Most of the submissions to CK are poetry, so try something different!

OUR IMPRESSIONS

Creative Kids is packed with a wide variety
of creative work (and incidentally, an amusing masthead). The editors occasionally
insert writing tips to accompany the stories
and other items. Departments like "Speak
Out" and "Write On" allow readers to voice
their opinions. This award-winning, profes-
sionally organized magazine was one of our
favorites to write for when we were grow-
ing up.

PUBLICATION	***Cricket***
ADDRESS	P.O. Box 300
	Peru, IL 61354
WEB ADDRESS	http://www.cricketmag.com
IN A NUTSHELL	This is a monthly full-color magazine for ages 9–14 containing fiction, poetry, and more. The magazine is 64 pages.
INDUSTRY PRESENCE	Established in 1973. Circulation: 60,000.
WORKS PUBLISHED	Although most of the magazine is written by adults, the monthly "Cricket League" contest (advertised in the magazine and online) allows readers to express their creativity through poetry, stories, art, and photography on specified topics. See magazine or Web site (click on "For Kids" at the top of the home page) for contest rules, themes, and deadlines.
THE ODDS	Approximately 3–5% of all contest submissions are published in the magazine, and another 5% are published online.
TIMELINE	Responds within a month after contest deadline.
RIGHTS AND COMPENSATION	Magazine takes all rights. Noncash prizes are awarded to winners. Two free copies for published authors, if requested.

SAMPLE COPY	Order at the above Web site for $4.95, or check your local library or bookstore.
SUBMISSION PROCESS	Mail to Cricket League at the address above. Do not e-mail submissions.
ADVICE FROM THE EDITORS	Editor Julie Peterson offers these reminders to contributors: "Be sure to stay within the word count limit. Every word counts except for the title. Be sure to follow contest rules . . . mail [your submission] in plenty of time for the entry to arrive by the deadline. We always get some very good entries that arrive too late to be considered. I suggest allowing a week within the U.S., just to be safe."
OUR IMPRESSIONS	*Cricket* is one of the most popular and well-known magazines for avid young readers. It offers plenty of stories and poems, as well as folk tales from various cultures, history pieces, and full-color illustrations. We love that *Cricket* respects young readers by defining potentially tough vocabulary words in the magazine's margins, rather than talking down to readers with overly simplistic language. Winning entries in the "Cricket League" contest, which are published in the back of the magazine, tend to be fanciful and humorous. In addition to *Cricket*, Carus Publishing produces sev-

eral other magazines on specific themes (*Cobblestone*, *Faces*, *Calliope*, and *Odyssey*, to name a few) that may also run contests from time to time. Check out the Web site for details.

PUBLICATION	**Faze**
ADDRESS	Faze Publications Inc.
	4936 Yonge Street, Ste. 2400
	Toronto, Ontario M2N 6S3
	Canada
	editor@fazeteen.com
WEB ADDRESS	http://www.fazeteen.com

IN A NUTSHELL This is a print and online general interest magazine for teens. The 68-page print edition is full-color, and is published 5 times per year.

INDUSTRY PRESENCE Established in 2000. Circulation 200,000.

WORKS PUBLISHED Print magazine includes news briefs, real-life stories, positive/empowering informative pieces, investigative reports, profiles of interesting people and celebrities, music reviews, and so forth. There is an online section for creative writing such as fiction, essays, book reviews, and poetry.

THE ODDS About 10% of submissions are accepted for publication in print and/or on the Web site.

TIMELINE Response time can be 2–3 months. The staff does not necessarily respond unless work is accepted.

RIGHTS AND COMPENSATION Authors retain the right to submit their pieces for publication elsewhere. Cash payment for articles published in the print magazine.

SAMPLE COPY

Contact the editorial offices.

SUBMISSION PROCESS

E-mail Editor-in-chief Lorraine Zander at editor@fazeteen.com with article ideas, or send manuscripts to webmaster@faze-teen.com for the online section.

ADVICE FROM THE EDITORS

The Web site boldly states, "*Faze* is a refreshing break from the standard dumbed-down teen magazines that only serve up regurgitated American pop culture and prom diet tips. *Faze* offers its readers insightful, hopefully inspiring looks at real life issues, youth culture, personal style, current affairs, real people, technology, travel, careers, health and fitness, and much more." Though mostly read by Canadians, *Faze* boasts loyal subscribers in the U.S., as well, and accepts submissions from teens worldwide. Executive Director Paul Zander says that 18- to 20-year-old writers generally achieve the most success with *Faze* and make up the core group of contributors. He recommends writing with a conversational tone, and being persistent in following up on the status of one's work. The magazine was originally created for both genders, but now its subscribers are primarily female. As a result, the editorial staff is planning to launch a magazine specifically for guys in the fall of 2006.

OUR IMPRESSIONS

We agree that *Faze* has found a way to stay in touch with pop culture without being a slave to it. The cover tends to feature musical artists of the day, but the magazine also offers world news, information on serious health issues, and sound advice for teens facing real-world problems like conflict with parents and bullies. Even the style and beauty section features photos of teens you might actually expect to see in your school, rather than the glossed-over models shown in most teen magazines. The articles also exhibit an underlying awareness of cultural differences and varying world views. The refreshingly blunt responses in the back-page Q & A section really tell it like it is.

PUBLICATION ADDRESS	***GUMBO*** 1818 N. Dr. Martin Luther King Dr. Milwaukee, WI 53212 tiffany@mygumbo.com
WEB ADDRESS	http://www.mygumbo.com
IN A NUTSHELL	This is a full-color magazine by and for teens, ages 13–19. It is 58 pages, and is published 6 times a year.
INDUSTRY PRESENCE	Established in 1998. Circulation: 25,000.
WORKS PUBLISHED	The kinds of articles that are typically found in youth magazines, on topics ranging from sports to health to celebrities to social issues—but all researched and written by teens. There's also a small poetry section.
THE ODDS	Magazine is 100% written by teens. Editors receive about seven queries per issue and accept about five of them, on average.
TIMELINE	Responds in 2–4 weeks. Lead time 4 to 6 months.
RIGHTS AND COMPENSATION	Authors retain the right to submit their pieces for publication elsewhere. Cash payment for published articles.
SAMPLE COPY	Mail $3 to address above.
SUBMISSION PROCESS	Send a one-page query letter describing your idea for an article and specifying whom you will interview for it or how

you plan to research it. Address queries to Tiffany Wynn, via mail to the address above, or e-mail to tiffany@mygumbo.com. E-mail is preferred.

ADVICE FROM THE EDITORS

Managing Editor Tiffany Wynn notes that common mistakes include wordiness, lack of transitions, and improper quotes. Be sure to keep your writing teen-focused, with a well-balanced viewpoint.

OUR IMPRESSIONS

Though celebrities are featured on the cover, the magazine mostly contains news and advice articles that send positive messages (like encouraging volunteer work) without preaching. The articles are better than the limited poetry. High school students in Milwaukee serve as editors and staff writers for *GUMBO*.

PUBLICATION	***New Moon: The Magazine for Girls and Their Dreams***
ADDRESS	2 W. First Street, #101 Duluth, MN 55802 girl@newmoon.org
WEB ADDRESS	http://www.newmoon.org
IN A NUTSHELL	This is a national magazine for girls age 8–14. It is primarily written by girls, as well, but does publish articles by female writers of all ages. The magazine has a two-color interior and a full-color cover. It is 56 pages in length, and there are 6 issues per year.
INDUSTRY PRESENCE	Established in 1993. Circulation: approximately 30,000.
WORKS PUBLISHED	By girls: fiction, letters, opinions, poetry, feature articles, personal essays, women's history pieces, and book reviews. By female writers of all ages: feature articles, history, and fiction. Upcoming themes are posted on the Web site with corresponding deadlines.
THE ODDS	At least 80% of every issue is written by kids or teens. Publishes approximately 5% of poetry and artwork received, 3% of fiction, and 10% of feature articles and department submissions.
TIMELINE	For artwork or poetry, the staff responds only if work is accepted. For other works,

the staff responds within 6 months to notify the writer of rejection or plans to hold the work for future consideration. Final decision may take up to 2 years (author is free to submit work elsewhere while waiting). After acceptance, *New Moon* generally collaborates with the author for 2–3 months to bring the manuscript from the submitted version to its final state.

Rights and Compensation

Generally buys all rights; may buy one-time rights if requested. Pays 6 cents per word for articles and stories and $10.00 for drawings and poetry. Also sends three contributors' copies to published authors.

Sample Copy

Order online at *New Moon* Web site for $6.75 (including postage), or check your local bookstore.

Submission Process

Mail or e-mail the Editorial Department at the addresses listed above. E-mail is preferred (no attachments). May query or send a complete manuscript.

Advice From The Editors

Assistant Managing Editor Lacey Louwagie writes, "We get a lot of stories from girls that clearly don't relate to the girl's life—for example, a 12-year-old will send us a story about a 22-year-old woman about to get married. . . . We prefer stories about girls the same age as our readers. The most compelling stories and articles are the ones that girls write based on their own experience or their own passions and interests. . . . We're always in need of good science articles, which include experiments. We love getting Herstory submissions, as well—interesting profiles of women from history. We appreciate stories that reflect the rich diversity of girls' lives and we love hearing from girls who live outside North America." In terms of the submission process, she says, "The most common mistake we see is girls leaving their contact information off their writing . . . your complete name, age, and address must be on there." To increase your chances of being published, Ms. Louwagie says, "Read copies of the magazine . . . [to] understand the type of work we print. *New Moon* covers a wide range of stories and articles, so I would suggest reading at least three issues . . . before you submit anything." The adult writers' guidelines also state that "an article written by a girl will always take precedence over an adult-written article of a similar nature."

OUR IMPRESSIONS

This is truly an exceptional magazine. The editorial staff celebrates girlhood and expresses a great deal of encouragement toward their readers and young writers. In fact, they believe so much in girls' abilities that the adult editors and the Girls Editorial Board share equally in the decision-making process (see Chapter 4 for an in-depth look at the GEB). A neat advice column allows readers to ask for and provide advice to each other, rather than having an adult respond to all the questions. *New Moon* celebrates variety in culture and background and gives girls ample opportunity to express their opinions and concerns about adolescence and community and social issues. Young writers may find it beneficial to read not just the girls' guidelines but the adult guidelines also, as they offer additional insights.

PUBLICATION ADDRESS	***Positive Teens*** c/o SATCH Publishing P.O. Box 301126 Boston, MA 02130-0010 info@positiveteensmag.com
WEB ADDRESS	http://www.positiveteensmag.com
IN A NUTSHELL	*Positive Teens* is an international full-color general-interest magazine by and for teens and young adults, ages 12–21. It is 30 pages, and there are 6 issues per year. Some submissions are printed online, as well.
INDUSTRY PRESENCE	Established in 1998. Circulation: 3,000–5,000 copies per year.
WORKS PUBLISHED	Articles, personal essays, poetry, artwork, and interviews.
THE ODDS	Approximately 70% of the magazine is written by teens and/or young adults. Publishes about 80% of submissions received.
TIMELINE	Responds in 4–8 weeks. Lead time is 2 to 3 months.
RIGHTS AND COMPENSATION	Magazine asks for exclusive use of accepted work for 18 months to reproduce, publish, and distribute materials. After this time, rights revert back to the author. Payment includes contributors' copy and $5 to $30.

SAMPLE COPY

Send $4.50 for a current issue or $3.00 for a back issue to the address above; also include $1.29 for postage. See order form online.

SUBMISSION PROCESS

Mail or e-mail Susan Manning, Publisher/Editor-in-chief, at the addresses above. E-mail should include the word "SUBMISSION" in the subject box.

ADVICE FROM THE EDITORS

Editor-in-chief Susan Manning writes, "Avoid copyright infringement of other people's work. . . . We prefer writers to choose their own topics and write about anything they think their peers would find interesting to read. Don't assume that what you have to say won't be interesting to others. Take a chance and send your work for review. Speak in [your] own voice when writing a nonfiction story and avoid writing in an authoritarian tone. Overuse of words and phrases such as: *you should*, *you must*, and *make sure to* are turn-offs for our publication. A writer should always submit his or her work either typed in black ink or handwritten in black or blue ink—not written in pencil. A submission should always include somewhere on the document the author's name, age, contact information, [and the date]."

OUR IMPRESSIONS

Because your chances of acceptance are relatively high, you may find *Positive Teens* to be a good starting point for publishing your writing. The photos and bios of contributing writers are a nice touch.

PUBLICATION ADDRESS	***Potluck Children's Literary Magazine*** P.O. Box 546 925 Holmes Avenue Deerfield, IL 60015 submissions@potluckmagazine.org
WEB ADDRESS	http://www.potluckmagazine.org
IN A NUTSHELL	This is a national literary magazine by and for writers and artists ages 8–16. It is black and white with a color cover. The magazine is 48 pages, and there are 4 issues per year.
INDUSTRY PRESENCE	Established in 1997. Circulation: 2,000.
WORKS PUBLISHED	Poetry, short stories, fables, book reviews, and artwork.
THE ODDS	95% of the magazine is written by kids and teens. Publishes 10–15% of the submissions received.
TIMELINE	Submission deadline for each issue is 3 months before the publication date (see Web site for details). Responds within 6 weeks after each deadline.
RIGHTS AND COMPENSATION	Magazine holds first rights. Payment includes contributor's copy.
SAMPLE COPY	$5.80, order by mail or by phone (see Web site for details). Also available in some bookstores.

SUBMISSION PROCESS

Mail or e-mail submissions to Susan Napoli Picchietti, Editor-in-chief at the addresses above.

ADVICE FROM THE EDITORS

Editor-in-chief Susan Napoli Picchietti offers this advice to writers, "Be yourself—write from your heart, your experiences, and be honest. [Avoid] explaining a story instead of telling a story . . . if you explain a story, the reader doesn't get to experience all the emotion and suspense the characters go through."

OUR IMPRESSIONS

We love their policy of responding to all submissions personally with critiques and encouragement. Although the staff reserves the right to edit work, the author's approval of the changes is obtained before printing the piece.

PUBLICATION	***Shameless***
ADDRESS	P.O. Box 68548
	360A Bloor St. W.
	Toronto, Ontario M5S 1X1
	Canada
	submit@shamelessmag.com; showandtell@
	shamelessmag.com
WEB ADDRESS	http://www.shamelessmag.com

IN A NUTSHELL — International Canada-based magazine for "smart, strong, sassy young women." Publishes work by all ages and both genders. The magazine is black and white with color cover. It is 48 pages and there are 3 issues per year.

INDUSTRY PRESENCE — Established in 2004. Circulation: approximately 2,000.

WORKS PUBLISHED — News briefs, reader profiles, interviews, personal essays, advice columns, feature articles, and reviews. Topics covered include current events, sociopolitical issues, and culture, among other things. The Show+Tell section is reserved for writing and artwork by teens and young adults.

THE ODDS — Approximately 10% of the magazine is written by teens. Publishes a small percentage of teen writing received.

TIMELINE	Response time is anywhere from 2 weeks to 3 months. Lead time is 4–5 months on average.
RIGHTS AND COMPENSATION	Magazine takes first publishing rights with the option to post the piece online, as well. Contributors receive a free copy of the magazine.
SAMPLE COPY	Order via Web site or mail. Single issue is $5 Canadian for residents of Canada, $8 Canadian for all others. Also available in some stores as listed on the Web site.
SUBMISSION PROCESS	Address query letters to Nicole Cohen and Melinda Mattos at submit@Shamelessmag. com. Send short Show+Tell items to showandtell@shamelessmag.com. E-mail is preferred, but mail may be sent to the address above.
ADVICE FROM THE EDITORS	Copublisher/Editor Nicole Cohen writes, "Please, read the writer's guidelines online before you submit. Often people submit entire stories, when all we want is a query. [Or they] pitch ideas without having ever picked up a copy of the magazine. It's important to know what types of [work] we publish, and what section you think your piece can go in."
OUR IMPRESSIONS	*Shameless* is an excellent addition to independent media. While currently most of

the writing is by "professional/emerging writers in their 20s and 30s," we get the impression that the editors would be happy to consider proposals from older teens, as well. Although they published few teen submissions in their first year, this was largely because teens tended to submit already-written pieces, rather than queries (which are preferred). In other words, if you are a relatively experienced teen writer (especially one with a few publishing credits), then go for it.

PUBLICATION ADDRESS	***Skipping Stones*** P.O. Box 3939 Eugene, OR 97403-0939 editor@SkippingStones.org
WEB ADDRESS	http://www.skippingstones.org
IN A NUTSHELL	This is an international multicultural magazine for readers age 8–16 that publishes work by all ages. It is black and white with a color cover. The magazine is 35 pages and there are 5 issues per year.
INDUSTRY PRESENCE	Established in 1988. Circulation: approximately 2,000.
WORKS PUBLISHED	Essays, stories, poetry, riddles and proverbs, games, quizzes, activities, photos, and artwork related to each issue's theme (see Web site). Writings accepted in all languages, with an English translation if possible. Suggested topics include multicultural understanding, international travel or living experiences, social responsibility, nature appreciation and conservation, personal growth, family issues, and equality.
THE ODDS	60–75% of the magazine is written by kids and teens. Publishes 10–15% of submissions received.
TIMELINE	Responds in 2–3 months. Lead time is 3–4 months.

RIGHTS AND COMPENSATION	Magazine holds first serial rights and reprint rights, but authors retain copyright and may submit work elsewhere after publication. Authors receive a contributor's copy.
SAMPLE COPY	Send $5 and your address to the editor.
SUBMISSION PROCESS	Mail or e-mail Mr. Arun Narayan Toké at the addresses listed above. Your e-mail should include your submission as a Microsoft Word document attachment.
ADVICE FROM THE EDITORS	Mr. Toké says to avoid fiction, love stories, or love poems that do not offer real insights or life lessons. Don't send chapter books with more than 1,000 words. Do include your complete home address and e-mail. *Skipping Stones* would like to receive more nonfiction, personal essays, opinion pieces, letters to the editor, puzzles, and cooperative games. The editors receive too many simplistic poems and stories without much substance to them.
OUR IMPRESSIONS	Mr. Toké refers to *Skipping Stones* as a "labor of love," and it shows. Their willingness to publish foreign-language submissions (alongside an English translation) is a unique treat. The editors are genuinely interested in the experiences and creative processes of all of their contribu-

tors. If possible, send illustrations or photos to enhance your story or essay; it may increase your chances of getting published. While some of the topics are serious, most of the magazine is refreshingly positive, a hopeful celebration of cultures.

CONTEST OPPORTUNITY

Skipping Stones holds the Annual Youth Honor Awards competition. Youth, ages 7–17, are invited to submit original writing (essays, interviews, poems, plays, short stories, etc.) and art (photos, paintings, cartoons, etc.) that promote multicultural and nature awareness. Ten winners are published in *Skipping Stones* and also receive a certificate, a subscription to the magazine, and five nature and/or multicultural books. See Web site for details.

Publication	***Stone Soup Magazine***
Address	P.O. Box 83
	Santa Cruz, CA 95063
Web Address	http://www.stonesoup.com
In a Nutshell	This is a 48-page, full-color literary magazine by and for young writers age 8–13. There are 6 issues per year.
Industry Presence	Established in 1973. Circulation: 20,000.
Works Published	Stories, poems, book reviews, and art.
The Odds	100% of the magazine is written by kids. Publishes less than 1% of submissions received (about 1 out of 300).
Timeline	Response time 4–6 weeks; only responds if interested in publishing the manuscript. Lead time is 4 months to 1 year.
Rights and Compensation	Normally purchases all rights, but willing to negotiate. Payment includes two contributor's copies and $40 ($25 for artwork).
Sample Copy	Order online or read highlights from past issues found on the Web site. Also available in many libraries and bookstores.
Submission Process	Mail to Submissions Department at the address listed above.
Advice From the Editors	Cofounder and editor Gerry Mandel stresses the importance of carefully following the guidelines and also reading past issues of

Stone Soup to get an idea of the kind of work that is published. Contributors are encouraged to "use your own experiences and observations to give your work depth and a sense of reality."

OUR IMPRESSIONS

Stone Soup is probably the most widely known by-kids-for-kids magazine in the United States, and is definitely a high quality publication. It encourages readers to send letters offering comments on specific works published in the magazine, which is helpful because peer feedback is so useful. However, they are only able to publish a tiny fraction of the work they receive (they get about 250 submissions per week!) and do not have the time and resources to respond to all submissions. Still, it's always worth a shot—to many young writers, *Stone Soup* is a very prestigious target.

PUBLICATION	***Teen Ink***
ADDRESS	P.O. Box 30
	Newton, MA 02461
	Editor@TeenInk.com
WEB ADDRESS	http://www.teenink.com
IN A NUTSHELL	A monthly print magazine and online magazine for teens, ages 13–19. The print magazine is 48 pages, and it is mostly black and white, with a few pages in full color.
INDUSTRY PRESENCE	Established in 1989. Circulation: more than 350,000.
WORKS PUBLISHED	Fiction, poetry, opinion, personal essays, articles, reviews (of books, music, movies, etc.), art, and photography.
THE ODDS	*Teen Ink* is 100% written by teens. About 5–10% of submissions are published in print, online, or both.
TIMELINE	May not respond to every submission received. Lead time ranges from a few weeks to 6–8 months.
RIGHTS AND COMPENSATION	Work published by *Teen Ink* may be submitted by the author for publication elsewhere. Complimentary copy for those published in print magazine.
SAMPLE COPY	Visit the Web site to request a sample issue of the print magazine.

SUBMISSION PROCESS

Mail to Editor at the address above, or submit online.

ADVICE FROM THE EDITORS

Pieces must be fewer than 2,500 words to be published. According to publisher John Meyer, *Teen Ink* receives lots of poetry and fiction, so the competition is toughest in those areas. Material like book and movie reviews and opinions on current events have the greatest chance of being published. The editors are always looking for more humor and fresh voices.

OUR IMPRESSIONS

Teen Ink is one of the best magazines of its kind. Topics in the magazine range from sports, to community service, to travel and culture. The print magazine has the look of a newspaper, but with a color cover and some color artwork on the inside. There are a few ads, but they don't overwhelm the reader. The Web site is colorful and easy to navigate, offering submission guidelines, writing tips, and a bulletin board in addition to lots more teen writing.

WORKSHOP OPPORTUNITY

Teen Ink offers a 2-week summer writing program in London. E-mail London@TeenInk. com for more info. The Web site also provides links to many other summer programs devoted to all kinds of activities, including writing.

Publication Address	***Teen Voices***
	80 Summer Street, Ste. 300
	Boston, MA 02110
	TeenVoices@TeenVoices.com
Web Address	http://www.teenvoices.com
In a Nutshell	This is a glossy full-color biannual print magazine and monthly online magazine by, for, and about teen women under age 18. It is 58 pages.
Industry Presence	Established in 1988. Circulation: 45,000.
Works Published	Fiction, poetry, articles, art, photography, comics, and more. Visit Web site for list of topics currently needed.
The Odds	90–95% written by teens. About 10–15% of submissions are published.
Timeline	Editors acknowledge receipt of submissions within a month. Manuscript is then filed, and author receives a response if and when the editors decide to use it.
Rights and Compensation	The author is welcome to submit the same piece to other markets at any time. Complimentary copies for those published in print magazine.
Sample Copy	Call 1-888-882-TEEN to request a sample copy for $5.

SUBMISSION PROCESS

Mail to Submissions Editor at the address above, or submit online.

ADVICE FROM THE EDITORS

Submissions should be written from a teen girl perspective (i.e., no adult or male protagonists). *Teen Voices* receives too many love poems, but short stories with a positive tone are always welcome. Editor-in-chief Ellyn Ruthstrom also says that she is "looking for first-person essays on a teen's personal thoughts about just about anything; we want to publish more of these on our Web site." Ms. Ruthstrom also requests that submissions include the writer's full name, age, mailing address, phone number, and e-mail if possible.

OUR IMPRESSIONS

Teen Voices balances thoughtful articles about social issues like teen activism with more light-hearted, entertainment-related topics. In general, it's more journalistic than literary. Underprivileged high school students in the Boston area help to edit the magazine, which emphasizes that each one of its readers is "more than just a pretty face." Although the staff welcomes submissions on any topic at any time, we recommend sending work that fits with upcoming themes announced on the Web site—otherwise you may be waiting a year or longer to see it published.

PUBLICATION	***Teen World News***
ADDRESS	teenworldnews@yahoo.com
WEB ADDRESS	http://www.teenworldnews.com
IN A NUTSHELL	An international online forum by and for teens.
INDUSTRY PRESENCE	Established in 2002.
WORKS PUBLISHED	Primarily news-related articles, social commentaries, and reviews; also publishes some poetry and short stories.
THE ODDS	100% written by teens. Publishes about 90% of submissions received.
TIMELINE	Responds within 2 weeks. Lead time up to a month (except for summer vacation).
RIGHTS AND COMPENSATION	Writers retain all rights to their work. No payment.
SUBMISSION PROCESS	E-mail to address above.
ADVICE FROM THE EDITORS	Editor Catherine Boalch writes, "The best way for teens to submit material is to read the site and get a sense of what the focus is. All the material should be accessible to a wide range of readers around the world, so if the article is on a topic very specific to one region or country, the writer should try to explain why it would be relevant or of interest to other teens. They should also bear in mind that for many of our readers,

English is their second language. So, simple, easy-to-understand articles are best. Proofread, please! We are happy to edit grammar of foreign writers, but we wish more American writers would put more effort into their copy before submitting it . . . shorthand and lingo are best avoided. Also, writers should be clear about what particular topic they are responding to—there are many questions and talkback forums on the Web site! Put the subject in the subject line [of your e-mail]. Nonfiction that gives a teen's perspective on a recent current event is the most appealing."

OUR IMPRESSIONS

Teen World News has a lot to offer as an international discussion forum for teenagers. The comments and personal essays literally come from students all over the world, with topics ranging from school uniforms to coping with discrimination, from favorite novels to beauty pageants, world politics, and everything in between. The site clearly focuses on teens sharing their views with each other, rather than on showcasing their writing ability per se. If you like to write straightforward, conversational prose about issues that concern you, you may find *Teen World News* appealing.

PUBLICATION	**Young People's Press**
ADDRESS	374 Fraser Street
	North Bay, ON P1B 3W7
	Canada
	submissions@ypp.net
WEB ADDRESS	http://www.ypp.net

IN A NUTSHELL

This is a free news service for teens and young adults, ages 14–24. Based in Canada, YPP has published young writers' articles in more than 500 newspapers in the U.S. and Canada, as well as on the Internet.

INDUSTRY PRESENCE

Established in 1996.

WORKS PUBLISHED

News articles, opinion pieces on youth issues, first-person essays, and the like—all nonfiction.

THE ODDS

Difficult to quantify. The editors indicate that about half of the submissions received are published on the Web site and/or in a newspaper. If you are flexible, your chances of being published will improve significantly (see below).

TIMELINE

Varies.

RIGHTS AND COMPENSATION

In most cases, authors are free to publish their work again elsewhere (ask first). Cash payment may or may not be available, depending on the newspaper that publishes the work.

SUBMISSION PROCESS

E-mail a story idea or an article you have already written to the address above. An editor will work with you via e-mail to help you get the article published on the Web site or in a newspaper such as the *Toronto Star*. Expect a response only if the editors are interested in the piece.

ADVICE FROM THE EDITORS

YPP receives a lot of first-person stories on social justice and teen issues (diary-type submissions). Feature articles that include interviews of other teens are in higher demand. Also take care not to "overwrite"; articles more than 600–800 words are more difficult to place. Be sure to include concrete examples to back up broader statements. Staffer Julie Crljen notes, "We can work with almost any submission, but oftentimes, the writer will choose not to work with the editors to change their submissions." In other words, you'll have a better shot at getting published if you are flexible about revisions to your work. Ms. Crljen adds: "Any article about a new or unknown trend, phenomenon, movement, [etc.] has a great chance of being published."

OUR IMPRESSIONS

This sounds like a wonderful opportunity to gain journalistic experience under the wing of a professional editor. YPP stories have run in a variety of newspapers, from small to large. An article with broad appeal (i.e., not a local news story) will probably have the best shot. The Web site, which is updated with student writing about once per week, offers useful tips on how to write opinion pieces and news articles, as well as a comprehensive manual on youth journalism, the YPP Writer's Guide.

MARKETS TO WATCH

Channel One Network

MARKET
WEB ADDRESS

http://www.channelone.com

WHAT WE KNOW

Channel One is a television news network specifically geared to young people. Established in 1990, it produces daily news broadcasts that are delivered to nearly 12,000 middle and high schools across the U.S. Their Web site has also showcased teen writing in the Student Exchange section. Content includes succinct, bullet-point style news articles, opinion articles on everything from smoking to travel tips, essays, stories, and poetry. Unfortunately, it appears that the Student Exchange section is no longer being updated on a regular basis. Only two or three news articles were posted in 2005, and there hasn't been a new short story since 2003.

PLANS FOR
THE FUTURE

Unknown. We were unable to reach anyone at Channel One to find out if they are still accepting submissions for the Student Exchange. Still, it can't hurt to send something in and see what happens.

MARKET
WEB ADDRESS

WHAT WE KNOW

PLANS FOR
THE FUTURE

Merlyn's Pen
http://www.merlynspen.org

When we were teens, *Merlyn's Pen* was one of our favorite markets, a monthly magazine of literary writing by and for middle school and high school students, first established in the late 1980s. Eventually it was reinvented as an annual anthology of student writing, and is now on hold. The Web site promises to be a top-notch resource for young writers, with writing tips, information on several writing camps and workshops, the Mentors in Writing Program (see Chapter 3), and a large collection of teen writing from past issues of the magazine. The Merlyn's Pen Foundation also holds occasional contests with cash prizes.

Editor Jim Stahl has indicated that another organization may resume publishing *Merlyn's Pen* and accepting submissions in 2006.

MARKET **WEB ADDRESS**	***Speak Up*** http://www.speakuppress.org
WHAT WE KNOW	*Speak Up* is a national literary journal by and for young adults, ages 13–19. In the past, it has been published annually and has included original fiction, essays, poetry, plays, and art. The journal also has both a local and an online Teen Advisory Board, whose members help to decide which submissions to publish.
PLANS FOR THE FUTURE	*Speak Up* did not accept new submissions in 2005. As of October 2005, the editors were "fairly sure" that the journal would be revived in a different format sometime in 2006. We certainly hope that it will. Judging from the sample issue we've seen, *Speak Up* is among the best of the publications dedicated to young writers. Keep checking the Web site for any news of its return.

MARKET **WEB ADDRESS**	***Student Bylines*** http://www.studentbylines.com
WHAT WE KNOW	Student Bylines has been published as a magazine by and for grades 6–12. At least one anthology of work—primarily poetry, short stories, and artwork—from the magazine has also been published. Unfortunately, the Web site was under construction when this book went to press.
PLANS FOR THE FUTURE	Unknown. However, since the anthology held promise, we recommend keeping an eye on this one.

MARKET **WEB ADDRESS**	***Teen Lit*** http://www.teenlit.com
WHAT WE KNOW	This is an online magazine, resource, and feedback forum for teen writers. The online magazine section, featuring student writing, has not been updated since late 2003. Fortunately, the discussion forums appear to be active. The Writers Workshop section still displays a few tips, but they are mostly brief nuggets of basic information.
PLANS FOR **THE FUTURE**	It looks like the site's founders, two high school teachers, are looking for student volunteers to take over maintaining the site. Check it out and get involved!

CONTESTS

CONTEST	***Achievement Awards in Writing***
ADDRESS	National Council of Teachers of English (NCTE)
	1111 W. Kenyon Road
	Urbana, IL 61801-1096
WEB ADDRESS	http://www.ncte.org
IN A NUTSHELL	This is an annual writing contest for high school juniors. Established in 1957.
ENTRY CONTENT	Requires two pieces of original writing: (1) an impromptu essay, written in 2 hours or less on a topic provided by NCTE, and (2) a 10-page prose or verse writing sample of your choice.
JUDGING	Entries are judged by high school and college English teachers, based on depth of thought in quality and presentation of ideas; student ownership of ideas; clarity of subject and audience; and command of vocabulary and sentence structure.
AWARDS	Winners receive certificates.
THE ODDS	Approximately 2,500 entries received.
SUBMISSION PROCESS	Requires nomination by English teacher.
TIMELINE	Nominations are due in late January, and entries are due in April. Winners are notified in October.

COMMENTS

The Web site offers additional contest information and a very helpful list of recent past topics for the impromptu essay. We highly recommend reviewing these so you will have an idea of what to expect.

Contest Address	***Ann Arlys Bowler Poetry Contest*** Weekly Reader Corporation 200 First Stamford Pl. P.O. Box 120023 Stamford, CT 06912-0023
Web Address	http://www.weeklyreader.com/teachers/ read/bowlers_con.asp
In a Nutshell	This is an annual poetry contest for students in grades 6–12. Established in 1989.
Entry Content	Up to three original poems of any genre, each one page or less.
Judging	Entries must show excellent command of English language, have spark, and appeal to middle school readers. Entries must not be previously published.
Awards	Winners receive $100, a medal, and publication in *Read* magazine. Semifinalists receive $50 and publication on *Read*'s Web site.
The Odds	Six winners and six semifinalists are selected.
Submission Process	Entries must be accompanied by an entry form, which requires parent signature and sponsoring teacher's signature.
Timeline	Deadline in late January. Winners are notified in April.

COMMENTS

Check out the What's Your Story section of the Weekly Reader Web site for other occasional writing contests offering cash prizes. The editorial staff also maintains a blog called "Word" that offers writing tips.

CONTEST	**Baker's Plays High School Playwriting Contest**
ADDRESS	Baker's Plays P.O. Box 699222 Quincy, MA 02269-9222
WEB ADDRESS	http://bakersplays.com and follow the link to "Play submissions"
IN A NUTSHELL	This is a playwriting contest for students in grades 9–12. Established in 1990.
ENTRY CONTENT	One or more plays of any length, about any subject, that could be produced by high school students on a high school stage.
JUDGING	Entries judged on originality and quality of writing appropriate for a high school audience. To appeal to a high school audience, plays should relate to the high school experience.
AWARDS	First place receives $500 and publication with a royalty-earning contract. Second place receives $250, and third place receives $100.
THE ODDS	Approximately 350 entries received.
SUBMISSION PROCESS	Mail to the address above. Requires teacher's signature.
TIMELINE	Deadline in late January. Winners are notified in May.

COMMENTS

Plays that have been production tested (i.e., through a public reading or full production) are preferable because they generally undergo revision during the rehearsal process. The Web site includes a catalogue of resources for budding playwrights.

CONTEST	**The Clarke-Bradbury International Science Fiction Competition**
ADDRESS	All information regarding this contest is available online.
WEB ADDRESS	http://www.itsf.org
IN A NUTSHELL	Annual science fiction writing and artwork contest. Established in 2003 to promote innovative ideas for future space technologies, and to recognize and pursue viable space technologies found in science fiction.
ENTRY CONTENT	Unpublished, original science fiction story (no more than 2,500 words) or creative artwork that incorporates the topic provided.
JUDGING	Entries are judged by a team of scientists and writers. Entries must show convincing use of technology, innovative ideas, and thinking "outside the box." For stories, the development of storyline, plot, and characters; clarity of expression; style; and degree of realism are also considered.
AWARDS	The winner in each category receives a cash prize of $600, and the runners-up in each category receive $300.
THE ODDS	Approximately 100 entries received in 2005.

SUBMISSION PROCESS	Entries must be submitted electronically, via e-mail or the Web site form.
TIMELINE	Deadline in late February. Winners are announced at Noreascon science fiction convention in September.
COMMENTS	Check the Web site for examples of past winners.

CONTEST	***Guideposts* Young Writers Contest**
ADDRESS	*Guideposts* Magazine
	16 E. 34th Street
	New York, NY 10016
WEB ADDRESS	http://www.guidepostsmag.com/young_writers_contest.asp
IN A NUTSHELL	This is a personal essay contest for students in grades 11 and 12. Magazine was established in 1945.
ENTRY CONTENT	Unpublished, true personal story (no more than 1,200 words), written in the first person, about an experience that deeply touched you or changed your life.
JUDGING	Entries are judged by the *Guideposts* editorial staff.
AWARDS	Authors of the top 10 manuscripts receive college scholarships ranging from $1,000 to $10,000. Ten honorable mentions receive $250 gift certificates for college supplies.
THE ODDS	*Guideposts* receives anywhere from 5,000 to 10,000 entries each year.
SUBMISSION PROCESS	Mail to the address above.
TIMELINE	Deadline in late November. Winners are notified by mail and announced in the June issue of *Guideposts*.

COMMENTS See the writer's guidelines on the Web site for additional suggestions on how to write your essay. Advice from the *Guideposts* staff: "Steer clear of writing about mission trips or deceased grandparents. This is one case in which it's okay to focus on yourself!"

CONTEST	**Laws of Life Essay Competition**
ADDRESS	John Templeton Foundation
	300 Conshohocken State Road, Ste. 500
	West Conshohocken, PA 19428
WEB ADDRESS	http://www.lawsoflife.org
IN A NUTSHELL	This essay competition is organized on a local level by schools and communities, usually for high school students. Established in 1987.
ENTRY CONTENT	An essay on any topic related to experiences and/or people that have shaped your values and your life.
JUDGING	Contest submissions are generally judged on compelling content, presentation, grammar, and spelling.
AWARDS	Prizes vary.
THE ODDS	Last year, more than 150,000 kids around the world wrote an essay.
SUBMISSION PROCESS	Varies locally.
TIMELINE	Check the Web site for participating contest locations and deadlines. Winners are announced at award ceremonies organized locally.
COMMENTS	The comprehensive Web site offers tips on how to get started and example essays written by other students.

CONTEST ADDRESS	**Letters About Literature Competition** LAL P.O. Box 609 Dallas, PA 18612
WEB ADDRESS	http://www.loc.gov/loc/cfbook/letters.html
IN A NUTSHELL	This annual letter-writing competition is for students in grades 4–12. Established in 1999.
ENTRY CONTENT	A personal letter (750 words or fewer) to an author, living or dead, from any genre, explaining how that author's work changed your way of thinking about the world or yourself.
JUDGING	Letters are judged on tone, organization, and expression of personal reaction to the author's book.
AWARDS	Cash prizes at state and national level.
THE ODDS	Unknown.
SUBMISSION PROCESS	Mail letter with entry coupon (see Web site for details).
TIMELINE	Letters are due in December. Winners are notified in March or April.
COMMENTS	Select a book you read recently that evoked strong feelings in you. You may not have liked the characters or the ending, but it

should be a book that affected you in some way. Write a letter to the author, making a connection between yourself and a character or event in the book. Avoid summarizing the plot of the book; focus on how it affected you. Be honest, personal, and conversational, as if the author were a friend who would write back to you.

CONTEST	**Manningham Student Poetry Awards**
ADDRESS	National Federation of State Poetry Societies
	501 Amsden
	Denison, TX 75021
WEB ADDRESS	http://www.nfsps.com/student_awards.htm
IN A NUTSHELL	This is an annual poetry competition for students in grades 6–8 (junior division) and 9–12 (senior division). Established in 1959.
ENTRY CONTENT	One poem of any subject and any form, up to 50 lines.
JUDGING	Poems are judged anonymously by a poet who is a member of the National Federation of State Poetry Societies. Poems with correct grammar, fresh images, meaningful content, and intriguing titles are most likely to be successful.
AWARDS	There are nine winners in each division. Cash prizes range from $10 for honorable mention to $75 for first prize. Winning poems are published in an anthology, of which the winning poets will receive a complimentary copy.
THE ODDS	Each state can submit a total of 10 poems per division.

SUBMISSION
PROCESS

Submit poem to state coordinator (see Web site).

TIMELINE

The deadline is in March, and winners are notified in May.

CONTEST	**NFAA Arts Recognition and Talent Search (ARTS) Awards**
ADDRESS	National Foundation for Advancement in the Arts 444 Brickell Avenue, P-14 Miami, FL 33131
WEB ADDRESS	http://www.nfaa.org
IN A NUTSHELL	This annual national arts scholarship program for high school seniors includes multiple categories, including writing.
ENTRY CONTENT	Participants can submit up to 6 poems, up to 3 short stories, up to 10 pages of a novel, up to 3 play scripts, or up to 3 essays.
JUDGING	Finalists attend ARTS Week, an all-expense-paid trip to Miami, FL, in January. During this event, finalists participate in classes, exhibitions, and workshops, and winners are selected. Submissions are judged against a standard of excellence, not against competing entries; hence, the number of winners is likely to vary from year to year.
AWARDS	Cash prizes range from $100 for merit awards to $10,000 for gold awards.
THE ODDS	There were about 1,000 entries and 54 merit award winners in the writing category in 2006.

SUBMISSION PROCESS	Register online, then submit work by mail for judging.
TIMELINE	See Web site.
COMMENTS	Check out the Web site for examples of writing submissions and winners from past years. With cash prizes of this size, competition will be tough.

Contest	**NFSPS College/University Level Poetry Awards**
Address	National Federation of State Poetry Societies N. Colwell Snell, Chairman P.O. Box 520698 Salt Lake City, UT 84152-0698
Web Address	http://www.nfsps.com/scholarship.htm
In a Nutshell	Poetry competition for students of accredited universities and colleges.
Entry Content	Manuscript of 10 poems (each no more than 46 lines), and notarized application.
Judging	Three judges select the highest quality pieces based on creativity, word usage, imagery, and mastery of form.
Awards	Cash prize of $500 for each winner. Winning manuscripts published by NFSPS, with 75 free copies for the author.
The Odds	Approximately 35 entries were received in 2005. There are two winners.
Submission Process	Mail to address above.
Timeline	The deadline is in February. Winners are announced after April 15.
Comments	The sponsors told us they would like to receive more entries, so go for it!

[NOT YOUR ORDINARY] DIRECTORY OF MARKETS · · · · · · · · · ·

CONTEST ADDRESS	**River of Words** P.O. Box 4000-J Berkeley, CA 94704
WEB ADDRESS	http://www.riverofwords.org
IN A NUTSHELL	This is an annual international environmental poetry contest for writers ages 5–19.
ENTRY CONTENT	Poem of no more than 32 lines. Multiple entries permitted.
JUDGING	Poetry judged by the River of Words cofounders: former U.S. Poet Laureate Robert Hass and writer Pamela Michael.
AWARDS	Winners attend the award ceremony at the Library of Congress in Washington, DC. Winning work is published on their Web site.
THE ODDS	Approximately 100 poems and artwork are selected as finalists.
SUBMISSION PROCESS	Mail submission to the address above, along with entry form. All entries become property of River of Words.
TIMELINE	The deadline is in mid-February. Winners are notified in April.
COMMENTS	According to the Web site, "The contest is designed to help youth explore the natural and cultural history of the place they live, and to express, through poetry and art,

what they discover." The site also includes
tips on writing poetry for the contest.

CONTEST ADDRESS	**The Scholastic Writing Awards** 557 Broadway New York, NY 10012
WEB ADDRESS	http://www.scholastic.com/artand writingawards
IN A NUTSHELL	This is an annual writing competition for students in grades 7–12. Established in 1923.
ENTRY CONTENT	Writing categories include poetry, short stories, dramatic scripts, personal essays, journalistic writing, and more. See Web site for details.
JUDGING	Entries are judged on technical proficiency, originality, and the emergence of a personal style or voice. Originality is essential.
AWARDS	National award recipients may have their work published in Scholastic magazines. Winners may receive a variety of prizes including cash awards, scholarships, and/or certificates.
THE ODDS	Approximately 250,000 entries received. There are more than 300 award recipients on the national level.
SUBMISSION PROCESS	Entries are submitted to regional affiliates first; regional winners go on to the national competition.

TIMELINE

Varies by region. Notification to regional award winners varies by region. National award recipients are notified in April.

COMMENTS

This is the largest student writing competition in the U.S., as you may have guessed from the number of entries received each year. On the plus side, a significant number of awards are also given. Check the Web site in October for the latest details about this year's competition. The Web site also includes numerous examples of previous award recipients' work in the Virtual Gallery.

Contest	**Student Science Fiction and Fantasy Contest**
Address	P.O. Box 314 Annapolis Junction, MD 20701
Web Address	http://www.bucconeer.worldcon.org/contest
In a Nutshell	This annual science fiction competition is for students in grades 5–12. Established in 1998.
Entry Content	Submit a science fiction/fantasy short story (50 pages maximum) and/or a factual science essay (35 pages maximum). See Web site for details.
Judging	Short story entries judged on originality, creativity, grammar and spelling, structure, character development, plot development, and use of science fiction and fantasy elements. Essay entries judged on content, grammar and spelling, structure, and use of references.
Awards	Semifinalists, finalists, and winners are invited to attend the science fiction convention, and bookstore gift certificates are awarded to finalists and winners.
The Odds	Approximately 500 entries are received.
Submission Process	Mail entry along with entry form from Web site to the address above.

TIMELINE Deadline is in March.

COMMENTS A selection of past winning entries are available on the contest's Web site.

CONTEST	**Young Playwrights Festival**
ADDRESS	National Playwriting Competition
	Young Playwrights Inc., Dept. WEB
	P.O. Box 5134
	New York, NY 10185
WEB ADDRESS	http://www.youngplaywrights.org/national-contest.htm
IN A NUTSHELL	This is an annual playwriting competition for students age 18 and younger. Established in 1981.
ENTRY CONTENT	One or more original plays of any style, subject, and length. Screenplays and musicals are not eligible. See Web site for details.
JUDGING	Entries are judged by theater professionals.
AWARDS	Winners participate in a writers' conference with professional theater artists in New York, and plays may be produced Off Broadway in the Young Playwrights Festival.
THE ODDS	Approximately 1,000 entries are received.
SUBMISSION PROCESS	Mail entry to the address above.
TIMELINE	Deadline is in December.
COMMENTS	The Web site offers lots of useful information about related opportunities such as workshops and summer programs to help interested students work through the process of writing a play.

NOTE ABOUT CONTESTS

There are numerous contests not listed here in detail because they are constantly changing; however, they are worth mentioning. For example, *Creative Kids*, The Merlyn's Pen Foundation, and *Byline Magazine* each hold various contests at various times throughout the year. (*Byline* only publishes winning contest entries by students and other work by adults; no unsolicited manuscripts are considered.) In order to learn about many such contests, you would probably need to subscribe to the host magazine. Otherwise, check your sample copies, the magazines' Web sites, or issues available at your library. Keep your eyes open for other notices, as well; some contests are announced in local newspapers, for example.

EPILOGUE

· · · · · · · · · · · · · · · · · ·

Though you are probably just beginning your foray into publishing, we'd like to offer some parting remarks about how your endeavors in writing and publishing can offer long-term benefits. We're not just talking about the prized bylines you will undoubtedly treasure for years to come. Writing well is a skill that will serve you throughout your lifetime, regardless of your chosen career path.

It may come in handy sooner than you think. Colleges and universities are always looking for prospective students who are committed to unique extracurricular activities, and publishing is certainly one of those. Though we have no way of knowing for sure, we believe that the publication of the first edition of this book helped us get accepted to Rice University. Titles like "published author" or "school newspaper editor-in-chief" can also make your resume stand out from the competition when you are applying for jobs. Why do admissions officers and employers find these qualifications so appealing? Because they indicate that you can not only communicate well, but also manage projects and deadlines, think creatively, and act as a leader.

If you sense in your heart (or your gut) that you want to be a professional writer some day, the benefits of getting a head start are fairly obvious. Still, even if writing never progresses beyond a hobby for you, the time you spend honing your craft will not go to waste. Many of our peers in high school predicted that we would both choose careers in journalism, but we ended up as engineers instead. (Yes, sometimes that seems weird to us, too.) Nevertheless, we both use our writing skills every day at our jobs—creating memos, technical reports, and other documents. (It's not always as dry as it sounds, and even when it is, at least our skills help us to complete those tasks quickly.) The ability to compose a concise and coherent argument or summary is an extremely valuable asset in just about any field. In a business environment, even an e-mail can carry a lot of significance, depending on the recipients. If you've been asked to send an update on a critical project to your boss's boss, you'll be grateful for your ability to communicate well, and he or she will appreciate it, too.

Even if your future day job involves too little writing for your tastes, you can keep your muse awake by continuing your freelancing, volunteering as editor for your favorite organization's newsletter, or writing a blog. So, go forth with confidence, and always leave a little room in your life for wordplay.

APPENDIX A: REGIONAL AND NATIONAL WRITING CAMPS

• • • • • • • • • • • • • • • • • • •

If you are really devoted to your writing and are looking for an immersion experience away from home, there are lots of regional and national writing camps in the U.S. The pages that follow present a sampling of writing camps from which to choose.

CAMP	**Aspen Summer Words**
PARTICIPANTS	All ages
LOCATION	Aspen, CO
DURATION	5 days in June
DESCRIPTION	This is a combination of a writing retreat, which includes workshops in fiction, poetry, magazine writing, and so forth, and a literary festival with author readings, panel discussions, and social gatherings. Aspen Summer Words celebrates the literature of various cultures. The opportunity exists for consultations with editors and agents, although there is an additional fee.
COST	Ranges from $150 for 2 days, up to $375 for the full workshop.
APPLICATION PROCESS	Requires writing samples and an application form.
WEB SITE	http://www.aspenwriters.org/summer.html
CONTACT INFORMATION	Phone: 970-925-3122; E-mail: info@aspenwriters.org

CAMP	**Duke Young Writers' Camp and Creative Writers' Workshop**
PARTICIPANTS	Grades 6–11 for the Young Writers' Camp and grades 10–11 for the Creative Writers' Workshop.
LOCATION	Duke University in Durham, NC
DURATION	12 days in June and July (three sessions offered for YWC, one for CWW)
DESCRIPTION	YWC: Students can choose among several classes on specific aspects of fiction, poetry, journalism, and playwriting. The daily readers' forum allows students to share their work with their peers. Morning and afternoon classes are offered, with free time for writing. Visit the Web site for a list of classes offered (varies each year). CWW: Intended for more advanced writers who want to refine their skills in a particular genre by building on works-in-progress, as well as starting new projects. Students get to select their primary instructor based on their specific interests. The workshop includes individual consultations with instructors.
COST	Ranges from approximately $750 for day campers to $1,500 for residential campers.

APPLICATION PROCESS	Students can register online beginning in December. CWW requires a writing sample.
WEB SITE	http://www.learnmore.duke.edu/Youth/programs.htm
CONTACT INFORMATION	Phone: 919-684-6259; E-mail: youth@duke.edu

CAMP	**Gotham Writers' Workshops**
PARTICIPANTS	Teen workshops are for students ages 11–14 and 15–18.
LOCATION	New York City and online
DURATION	Varies; 4 weeks in New York in the summer, or 8 weeks online
DESCRIPTION	Small classes (no more than 18 students) are taught by professional writers in a noncompetitive atmosphere. A wide variety of classes are offered.
COST	Approximately $350.
APPLICATION PROCESS	Register online or by calling 877-WRITERS
WEB SITE	http://www.writingclasses.com
CONTACT INFORMATION	Phone: 877-WRITERS

CAMP	**Idyllwild Arts Summer Program in Creative Writing**
PARTICIPANTS	Students ages 14–18.
LOCATION	San Jacinto Mountains, southern California
DURATION	2 weeks in July and August
DESCRIPTION	Separate workshops in fiction, poetry, and playwriting are offered for students at all levels of ability and experience. Students have individual conferences with instructors, and the program culminates in a student reading at the end. According to the program Web site, "This immersive program, while demanding, provides a competition-free environment. An exceptional faculty works closely with each student, stressing individual growth while encouraging achievement."
COST	$2,050 including room and board.
APPLICATION PROCESS	Students complete an application form and submit a teacher recommendation.
WEB SITE	http://idyllwildarts.org
CONTACT INFORMATION	Phone: 951-659-2171; E-mail: summer@idyllwildarts.org

Camp	**Interlochen Arts Camp**
Participants	Students in grades 9–12.
Location	Interlochen, MI
Duration	3 weeks in the summer
Description	The creative writing program consists of separate sessions on narrative and verse, dramatic writing, poetry, and fiction. According to the program Web site, "Interlochen's Creative Writing programs will provide students with an intensive three-week immersion in the world of writing. Students will work under the apprenticeship of professional writers and teachers on an individual basis. Guided writing assignments, reading assignments, visiting guest writers, discussion and critique are part of the daily curriculum. Students will present weekly public readings."
Cost	$3,150 including room and board; financial aid is available.
Application Process	Students complete an application form, and submit writing samples (depending on the session selected) and an essay explaining interest in writing and in the program.
Web Site	http://www.interlochen.org/camp
Contact Information	Phone: 231-276-7472; E-mail: admissions@interlochen.org

CAMP	**Kent School Summer Writers Camp**
PARTICIPANTS	Students in grades 8–10.
LOCATION	Kent, CT
DURATION	3 weeks in July
DESCRIPTION	This camp offers classroom and workshop instruction in creative writing, with a total of about 50 students. Students explore narrative, poem, and essay writing in all stages of the writing and editing process. Individual and group feedback are offered, and students can share their work in a "coffee house" atmosphere.
COST	$2,375 including accommodations.
APPLICATION PROCESS	Students admitted on first-come, first-served basis; A writing sample, school transcript, and letter of recommendation are required.
WEB SITE	http://www.writerscamp.org
CONTACT INFORMATION	Todd Marble; Phone: 860-927-6038; E-mail: marblet@kent-school.edu

CAMP	**Sewanee Young Writers Conference**
PARTICIPANTS	Students in grades 9–12.
LOCATION	University of the South in Sewanee, TN
DURATION	First 2 weeks in July
DESCRIPTION	Students participate in small workshops in fiction, poetry, and creative nonfiction. Other highlights include lectures by the university's English faculty; readings by teachers, peers, and visiting writers; one-on-one conferences with instructors; and meals with visiting authors.
COST	$1,450 including room and board.
APPLICATION PROCESS	A letter of recommendation from a teacher and a writing sample are required.
WEB SITE	http://www.sewanee.edu/ywc
CONTACT INFORMATION	Elizabeth Grammer, director; Phone: 931-598-1541; E-mail: egrammer@sewanee.edu

CAMP	**Writers Workshop at Susquehanna University**
PARTICIPANTS	Students entering grades 11–12.
LOCATION	Susquehanna University in Selinsgrove, PA
DURATION	1 week in June and July
DESCRIPTION	Offers intensive, small-group workshops in fiction, creative nonfiction, and poetry, headed by nationally recognized authors, as well as individual conferences with instructors, public reading of students' writing at the end of the workshop, and publication in a Writers Workshop magazine.
COST	Approximately $500 including room and board on campus.
APPLICATION PROCESS	Students submit teacher/counselor recommendations and a writing portfolio.
WEB SITE	http://www.susqu.edu/writers/ HighSchoolStudents.htm
CONTACT INFORMATION	Dr. Gary Fincke, director; Phone: 570-372-4164; E-mail: writerswork@susqu.edu

APPENDIX B:
BOOK PUBLISHING
OPPORTUNITIES

• •

CONTESTS

CONTEST	**Annual David Melton Memorial Written & Illustrated By . . . Contest for Students**
ADDRESS	Landmark Editions 1904 Foxridge Drive Kansas City, KS 66106
WEB ADDRESS	http://www.landmarkeditions.com
INFORMATION	Formerly known as the National Written and Illustrated By . . . Awards Contest, the program breaks down into three categories according to the author's age: ages 6–9, 10–13, and 14–19. Each year, one storybook from each category is selected for

publication. However, there are two caveats: First, the book must also be illustrated by the author. (Thankfully for those of us whose drawing skills begin and end with stick figures, original computer graphics and photographs are allowed.) Second, the target audience of the book must be ages 5–9, regardless of the author's age. For complete contest rules and guidelines, visit the Web site.

CONTEST	**Annual Delacorte Dell Yearling Contest for a First Middle-Grade Novel and Annual Delacorte Press Contest for a First Young Adult Novel**
ADDRESS	Delacorte Yearling Contest Random House, Inc. 1745 Broadway, 9th Floor New York, NY 10019
WEB ADDRESS	http://www.randomhouse.com/kids/ writingcontests
INFORMATION	The purpose of the middle-grade novel award is to encourage writers to write a contemporary or historical fiction novel set in North America for readers ages 9–12. Likewise, the young adult novel award is meant to encourage the writing of contemporary young adult fiction for ages 12–18. In both cases, only writers who have not previously published a novel for the target age group are eligible for the award. First prize is a book contract, including advance and royalties.

CONTEST **Annual Lee & Low New Voices Award**
ADDRESS Lee & Low Books
95 Madison Avenue
New York, NY 10016
WEB ADDRESS http://www.leeandlow.com/editorial/
voices.html

INFORMATION The purpose of the New Voices Award is to recognize writers of color who create children's picture books. The winner must be a U.S. resident and must not have previously published a picture book. The grand prize is a cash grant of $1,000 and a standard publication contract with Lee & Low Books. Although the contest is not specifically for teen writers, the publisher is willing to consider student submissions. As with the David Melton Memorial contest discussed above, the book does have to be written for a younger audience: in this case, ages 2–10. The book can be fiction or nonfiction.

CONTEST
ADDRESS

Annual PUSH Novel Contest
c/o The Scholastic Art & Writing Awards
557 Broadway
New York, NY 10012-3999

WEB ADDRESS

http://www.thisispush.com

INFORMATION

One of many categories in the Scholastic Art & Writing Awards, the Novel Contest is open to students in grades 7–12. One winner is chosen each year and offered the opportunity to work with PUSH editors toward possible publication. See the Web site for contest deadline and details.

CONTEST **Kids Are Authors**

ADDRESS Scholastic Book Fairs
1080 Greenwood Blvd.
Lake Mary, FL 32746

WEB ADDRESS http://teacher.scholastic.com/activities/kaa

INFORMATION This is an annual book competition for students in kindergarten through grade 8. Entries consist of a fiction or nonfiction picture book, 21–29 pages, written and illustrated by three or more students. Contest submissions are judged on originality, content, overall appeal to children, quality of artwork, and compatibility of text and illustrations. Two grand-prize winners (one fiction, one nonfiction) will be published by Scholastic Books and distributed at book fairs around the country. The contest sponsors recommend reviewing previous winners for inspiration. The Web site includes helpful tips for both the text and illustrations.

MAINSTREAM
BOOK PUBLISHERS

There are a number of mainstream publishers that have printed books by teens in the past or have advertised a willingness to do so in the future. They don't necessarily make a point of it (i.e., most of their books are by adults), but at least they may be open to the idea. Such publishers include:

Beyond Words Publishing, Inc.

Acquisitions Editor
20827 NW Cornell Road, Ste. 500
Hillsboro, OR 97124-9808
http://www.beyondword.com

Free Spirit Publishing

Attn: Acquisitions
217 Fifth Avenue North, Ste. 200
Minneapolis, MN 55401-1299
http://www.freespirit.com

Penguin Group (USA)

Note: The Penguin Group publishes books under many different imprints, among them New American Library. NAL publishes books for adults, including *Breaking the Code*, which was written by teens. Penguin Group imprints do not normally accept unsolicited submissions, but on rare occasions, the Web site will feature a listing of the imprints that may be willing to accept this type of work.

For adult imprints (including NAL):
375 Hudson Street
New York, NY 10014
http://www.penguin.com

For juvenile imprints:
345 Hudson Street
New York, NY 10014
http://www.penguin.com

ADDITIONAL RESOURCES

• • • • • • • • • • • • • • • • • • • •

Although we have done our best to sum up what you need to know to be a successful young writer, we haven't said it all. For more advice on writing itself, as well as publishing, check out the resources listed below, and browse your local library or bookstore.

BOOKS

Brogan, K. S. (2006). *Writer's market*. Cincinnati, OH: Writer's Digest Books. (Note: This book is updated annually, so be sure to look for the most current version.)

Brownstone, D. M, & Franck, I. M. (1999). *The complete self-publishing handbook: A step-by-step guide to producing and marketing your own book*. New York: Plume.

King, S. (2000). *On writing: A memoir of the craft*. New York: Scribner.

Larsen, M. (2004). *How to write a book proposal* (3rd ed.). Cincinnati, OH: Writer's Digest Books.

Pope, A. (Ed.). (2006). *Children's writer's and illustrator's market*. Cincinnati, OH: Writer's Digest Books. (Note: This book is updated annually, so be sure to look for the most current version.)

Poynter, D. (2003). *The self-publishing manual: How to write, print and sell your own book*. Santa Barbara, CA: Para Publishing.

Ross, T., & Ross, M. (2002). *The complete guide to self-publishing, 4th edition: Everything you need to know to write, publish, promote, and sell your own book*. Cincinnati, OH: Writer's Digest Books.

Strunk, W., Jr., & White, E. B. (2000). *The elements of style* (4th ed.). New York: Longman.

Truss, L. (2004). *Eats, shoots, & leaves: The zero tolerance approach to punctuation*. New York: Gotham.

Zinsser, W. (2006). *On writing well: The classic guide to writing nonfiction*. New York: HarperCollins.

WEB SITES

Byline **Magazine**
http://www.bylinemag.com

This monthly print magazine offers plenty of tips and advice for beginning writers of poetry, fiction, and nonfiction including listings of markets and writers' conferences and personal accounts from successful writers. At $24 for 11 issues, it's worth subscribing to this one. For a taste of what you'll be getting, check out the Web site. *Byline* runs several writing contests each year with (small) cash prizes and has a page devoted specifically to student writing, so it can be considered a market, as well.

Creative Writing for Teens

http://teenwriting.about.com

This site provides writing exercises and advice specifically geared toward teen writers. It also includes a forum for submitting and critiquing each other's work.

Elite Skills

http://www.eliteskills.com

This is a forum where writers can critique each other's work. Though intended for all ages, it's set up so that you can exchange feedback with others at the same age or experience level. Contributors are required to provide comments of a minimum length to discourage the "nice job" phenomenon—too brief, nonspecific assessments. The site includes mostly poetry but also some short stories.

Gotham Writers' Workshop

http://www.writingclasses.com

The home page of this site is very dense but well organized; if you take your time exploring it, you'll find a wealth of resources at your fingertips. Gotham offers several writing workshops both in New York City and online (see Appendix A for details), as well as a "story doctoring" critique service. The Writers' Toolbox includes quick tips and full articles by workshop faculty on specific aspects of writing, such as how to compose a compelling opening for your short story, or how to choose between the first person and the third person for a particular narrative. Looking for a book on how to write mysteries, or another market directory? Gotham offers a comprehensive list of other resources you can check out at your local library or bookstore. You can even order DVDs in which successful writers and editors will guide you through the revision process or the submission process.

The Rejection Collection
http://www.rejectioncollection.com

This unique site offers a forum for writers to commiserate on their rejection letters by sharing their tales of woe. If you feel the need to vent, this is the place. Inspirational accounts reveal how writers can use rejection as a motivator to turn their work around.

The Scriptorium
http://www.thescriptorium.net/youth.html

The Scriptorium offers advice for writers of all ages, and specifically for young writers, on topics such as writer's block and the essential elements of a story (characters, dialogue, etc.), which is particularly useful for beginners. There's also an online workshop and suggested writing exercises. The Web site is updated monthly.

Teen Ink
http://www.teenink.com

In addition to being a wonderful market for teen writing, the *Teen Ink* Web site includes a lengthy list of links to other helpful sites—from online dictionaries and grammar guides, to the American Society of Newspaper Editors, if you want to explore a career in journalism. You'll also find a list of other potential markets for your work. From the *Teen Ink* home page, click on the Resources link on the left-hand side to get started.

Writing magazine
http://www.weeklyreader.com/teens/writing

Weekly Reader publishes *Writing* magazine in addition to *READ* magazine. The Web site for *Writing* provides student contests, writing activities for practice, and a blog called Word. The blog includes tips on writing and publishing, as well as an interactive story allowing readers to submit suggestions for the next plot development. Teens can also submit their poetry, fiction, and nonfiction to *Writing* and *READ* through the site.

ABOUT THE AUTHORS

. . . .

Jessica Dunn and Danielle Dunn were eighth graders at Dulles Middle School in the Houston area when they began writing the first edition of this book, published in 1996. At that time, they had been freelance writers for magazines featuring young writers for 4 years. The twin sisters graduated from Rice University in 2003 with bachelor's degrees in chemical engineering.

Danielle works for a vaccine manufacturer in Pennsylvania, where she enjoys the summer festivals, fall colors, and the outlet malls. Her hobbies—aside from writing, of course—include traveling as often as her budget and vacation time will allow, singing in the car, and bowling (despite her utter lack of skill).

Jessica works in insulin manufacturing and lives in Indiana, where she envies Danielle's proximity to New York City. When not working, writing, or traveling, Jessica is busy designing an alternate universe in which all chocolate is dark chocolate, cluttered apartments clean themselves, and her car knows exactly where it's going at all times (because she sure doesn't).

To satisfy the curious, the twins would like to clarify that they were not able to communicate by telepathy in order to write this book. It might have worked across one state line, but Ohio got in the way.